CONTENTS

Chapter One: Families in the UK Today

Chapter Two: Parenting Issues

Introduction

Parenting is the sixty-seventh volume in the **Issues** series. The aim of this series is to offer up-to-date information about important issues in our world.

Parenting examines families in the UK today and parenting issues.

The information comes from a wide variety of sources and includes:
Government reports and statistics
Newspaper reports and features
Magazine articles and surveys
Web site material
Literature from lobby groups
and charitable organisations.

It is hoped that, as you read about the many aspects of the issues explored in this book, you will critically evaluate the information presented. It is important that you decide whether you are being presented with facts or opinions. Does the writer give a biased or an unbiased report? If an opinion is being expressed, do you agree with the writer?

Parenting offers a useful starting-point for those who need convenient access to information about the many issues involved. However, it is only a starting-point. At the back of the book is a list of organisations which you may want to contact for further information.

*****

What makes a family today?

Information from Familyonwards

By Jill Curtis

When I was researching for my book *Making and Breaking Families*, 'What makes a family today?' was a question I posted on the Internet and which appeared in several magazines and newspapers. I was overwhelmed by the huge response I received. It seemed that everyone had an opinion, and everyone wanted to tell me about the blueprint which they saw as 'making a family today'.

The exciting thing was, though, that the answers were varied and different. The contributions I read began to reflect the variety of groups which go to constitute a family at the end of the nineteen-nineties.

For many people, the word 'family' conjures up the traditional picture of two parents, usually married, and their children. How realistic is it to expect families to be like this now and in the future?

Of course, the media love to dwell on the number of broken families that there are. Statistics about the number of single-parent

families, blended and stepfamilies are there for us all to see. Quite often, though, the couples who have stayed together are sidelined, and they do not make the news. Yet there are families who have weathered storms, held fast together and are able to provide a safe untroubled harbour for the children over many years.

> *For many people, the word 'family' conjures up the traditional picture of two parents, usually married, and their children*

It seems to be a common cry from those married for thirty, forty or more years that the couples marrying today often see divorce as an easy way out, and that more should be spoken about the need to work at a relationship. Once the honeymoon is over, where do you go from there? Couples who had been married for years were pleased to have their opinions listened to. 'Be open and affectionate in front of the children'; 'Learn to say sorry and mean it'; 'Be independent at times, and dependent at others'; 'Take time to decide on marriage and then make it work' and, perhaps most telling of all, 'It doesn't just happen, make it happen.'

But, a wider chorus of voices made themselves heard and in my book I have tried to represent many different points of view. What of the men and women who have to 'go it alone'? Perhaps the reluctant partner in a divorce. The poor publicity given to 'single parents' makes their job even harder. What of the stepmother or stepfather trying to create a new and loving home for the children? They, too, have to cross public opinion while forging new relationships with children and a new partner. What of blended families, where couples who already have children come together to create a new family? We must acknowledge the fact there are grandparents parenting their grandchildren, often coming to the rescue after a family crisis. Finding yourself a parent 'second time around' is no easy task. There are gay and lesbian couples who parent a child, perhaps from an earlier heterosexual relationship.

The kaleidoscope of families is almost endless, but each in their own way hold on to beliefs about the family and what it stands for. A family, whatever the makeup, is about love and care and watching out for each other. I heard from Molly, now in her eightieth year: 'I am an old lady now, but I do know this. Families are all about care and must be a place to protect the young and the old, and the sick.'

The family may not be as recognisable as it once was, but it still thrives in a variety of ways. As well as the old, there are new patterns, and we must learn to recognise them and to support and to value them.

■ The above information is from Familyonwards's web site which can be found at www.familyonwards.com

© Jill Curtis 2001

The changing face of UK families

The old adage of keeping up with the Joneses is set to become a case of keeping up with Bridget Jones as the traditional family unit is replaced by a society of singletons.

According to new research from Abbey National, 2001 marked a turning point for the typical UK family: for the first time in history, people living on their own outnumbered traditional family households.

The findings predict that within five years childless couples living together will also outnumber family residences – yet just 40 years ago the family unit (couples with dependent children) made up half of all households in the UK.

The results are part of ongoing research for Abbey National and are designed to help the bank fully understand working families and develop flexible financial products to suit their lifestyles. Researchers quizzed three generations of families on their attitudes to family, finances and parenting.

Although there may be fewer traditional family households in the UK, relationships appear closer than ever before. Families are actually spending significantly more time together than past generations. Excluding time spent eating together, today's parents spend an hour and a half a day with their children compared with only a third of that (31 minutes) in 1961.

More good news for guilt-ridden modern parents is that of the total time spent with children, time spent caring for them has more than doubled from 30 minutes a day in 1961 to 75 minutes today. In addition, conscientious parents now spend an average of 15 minutes a day helping their children with homework compared with virtually no time in 1961.

Interestingly, for such a time-conscious generation, cooking habits have also altered: almost a fifth of all families today sit down to a home-cooked dinner every night of the week (at 5pm) compared with only 12 per cent of families in the 1960s.

> *Our findings point to an interesting paradox: as singleton and childfree family units fast become the norm, there are fewer families in the traditional sense of the word*

Janet Connor, Abbey National Retail Marketing Director, said: 'Our findings point to an interesting paradox: as singleton and childfree family units fast become the norm, there are fewer families in the traditional sense of the word. However, the conventional family – albeit there are less of them – is perhaps a closer unit than ever before with more quality time spent on parenting and relationships. The changing shape of the UK family means businesses and society will need to carefully reappraise their understanding of family life.'

Despite the increase in time spent with children, parents today have also created more time for themselves with the use of time-saving technologies and by the outsourcing of domestic chores. In 1961 cleaning and laundry took up a whopping 12 hours and 40 minutes of a woman's week. Today this has halved to six hours and 8 minutes.

Parents today are using this extra time to enrich their life with an ever-increasing variety of activities: time spent on sport and exercise is up from a mere 10 minutes a week 40 years ago to an hour a week today.

Time spent cooking has decreased for Mums, down from more than one hour and forty minutes in 1961 to just over an hour (73 minutes) today. At the same time, Dads have actually marginally increased their time in the kitchen from 26 to 27 minutes per day. And time spent entertaining friends and family at home has doubled from 25 minutes a week in 1961 to close to an hour (55 minutes) today.

■ The above information appeared on the Future Foundation's web site: www.futurefoundation.net

Households by size

The types of household people live in are now more varied than in the past. Where once people lived with their parents until marriage, increasingly people spend time living on their own, whether before or instead of marriage/cohabitation or as a result of divorce or the breakdown of a relationship.

Great Britain					Percentages
	1961	1971	1981	1991	2001[1]
One person	14	18	22	27	29
Two people	30	32	32	34	35
Three people	23	19	17	16	16
Four people	18	17	18	16	14
Five people	9	8	7	5	5
Six or more people	7	6	4	2	2

1 At Spring 2001

Source: Census: Labour Force Survey, Office for National Statistics

Birth rate drops to the lowest on record

As mothers leave it late, average family has 1.64 children

Birth rates in Britain have dropped to a historic low with women having an average of 1.64 children, official figures showed yesterday.

The statistics for last year also show that they are leaving it later and later before starting a family.

There were 595,000 children born in England and Wales in 2001, down 2 per cent on the year before, leading to the lowest birth rate since records began in 1924.

Analysts warn that, combined with longer life expectancy, this means there will be more pensioners than under-16s by 2007.

It also means that without immigration – currently at record levels – the population would be falling as a birth rate of 2.1 children per woman is needed to keep it stable.

The Office for National Statistics said the number of babies born has been falling steadily since 1991. Studies have also shown that one in five women is likely to remain childless.

The situation is even more serious elsewhere in Europe and has prompted some experts to warn of a 'population crisis'.

In Italy and Spain, birth rates have fallen to 1.2 children per woman.

In Germany the figure is 1.3 while it is 1.4 in Greece and 1.5 in Switzerland. France and Denmark have a rate of 1.7 children per woman and in Ireland it is just over 2.

The ONS report said the most significant influence on birth rates was the decision by women and their partners to have children later in life.

The average age of mothers-to-be has risen from 27 to 29. Although most were still having children aged 25 to 29, more babies were being born to mothers in their early 30s than in their early 20s.

By Jo Butler, Home Affairs Correspondent

Women living in London and the South-East were most likely to have a baby in their early 30s while elsewhere in the country, women aged 25 to 29 had the highest birth rates.

> *There were 595,000 children born in England and Wales in 2001, down 2 per cent on the year before, leading to the lowest birth rate since records began in 1924*

Another significant trend is a huge rise in multiple births, fuelled by a growing number of women undergoing fertility treatment.

In 2001, 8,484 women gave birth to twins, 211 to triplets and five had four or more babies at once. Many of the multiple births were among married women aged over 35.

The report also revealed a rise in the number of abortions as more than one in five conceptions ended in a termination last year.

In London, that figure rose to nearly one in three.

There was a very small drop in the number of pregnancies among 15- to 17-year-olds from 45 conceptions per 1,000 to 43.8. Of these pregnancies, 44 per cent were aborted.

The highest teenage birth rates were in the North-East and Wales, with the lowest in the South-East. Despite the falling birth rate, analysts believe the population in the UK will still rise in coming years, fuelled by higher immigration.

The population is likely to jump from just under 60 million in 2000 to 65 million by 2025, with 3.4 million of the rise coming from abroad.

© The Daily Mail, December, 2002

Diverse family forms across Europe

'British men in their mid-twenties are nearly five times as likely as Italian men to be living with a partner.'

New ESRC research highlights the diversity of family forms across the European Union. The study, specially commissioned for the ESRC's sixth national social science conference, was prepared by Professor Richard Berthoud and Dr Maria Iacovou, of Essex University's Institute for Social and Economic Research (ISER). The research is based principally on analysis of a survey of 73,000 households across the EU. Its findings include:

- In Finland, half of all young men have left the parental home before age 22. But in Italy, almost half of all men are still living with their parents by age 30. In the UK, the 'half-way' mark for men leaving home is 23.5.
- In all countries, women leave home earlier than men.
- Ireland has the largest households, with four people on average. In the UK, average household size is 2.8 and Sweden has the smallest households with an average size of 2.2.
- Between the ages of 23 and 27, only 9 per cent of Italian men are in partnerships, while 42 per cent of men in the UK have a partner: thus, British men are nearly five times as likely as Italian men to be living in a partnership in their mid-twenties.
- The most delayed fertility is in the Netherlands and Italy (with only around half of women in these countries having had a child by age 30), while the earliest fertility is in the UK and Austria (where half of all women are mothers by age 27). Indeed, early fertility in the UK is the highest in Europe, not just in the teenage years, but throughout the early twenties.
- In the southern countries, 33% of women over age 65 live with one or more of their children; in the north/central group only 10% live with a child; and in the Nordic countries, only 3% live in the same house as one of their children.

Between the ages of 23 and 27, only 9 per cent of Italian men are in partnerships, while 42 per cent of men in the UK have a partner

---

- Annual teen birth rates range from 6 per 1000 women in the Netherlands up to 30 per 1,000 women in the UK.
- Older people may move in with their adult children in order to be cared for by their children. But cohabitation between generations is not simply a case of the younger generation caring for their elderly parents: the older generation also helps the younger generation by providing childcare. There is far more reciprocity in such arrangements where the elderly co-resident is female: older men receive just as much care as older women, but they provide very little childcare.

- The above information is from the Economic and Social Research Council's web site which can be found at www.esrc.ac.uk

© Economic and Social Research Council (ESRC)

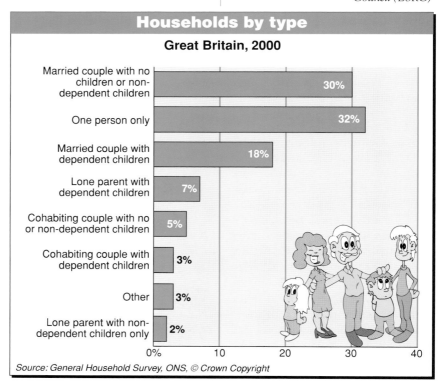

Households by type

Great Britain, 2000

Household type	Percentage
Married couple with no children or non-dependent children	30%
One person only	32%
Married couple with dependent children	18%
Lone parent with dependent children	7%
Cohabiting couple with no or non-dependent children	5%
Cohabiting couple with dependent children	3%
Other	3%
Lone parent with non-dependent children only	2%

Source: General Household Survey, ONS, © Crown Copyright

Nuclear family goes into meltdown

Generations learn to link up to cope with lonely lifestyle

By John Arlidge

The nuclear family of mum, dad and 2.4 kids is splitting up. Researchers have coined a name for the emerging British household – the Beanpoles. They 'live together' and have 1.8 children.

As Britons live longer, divorce rates rise and couples have fewer children, the traditional family – married parents with two or more children – is giving way to cohabiting couples with a single child.

A new study by the London-based research group Mintel shows family groups are getting 'longer and thinner – like a beanpole'. While 20 years ago the average extended family comprised three 'nuclear' generations, family groups are now made up of four generations of often cohabiting couples, each with an average 1.8 children.

'The family is undergoing radical changes under the pressure of an ageing population, longer lifespans, increased female working, the tendency to marry later in life, the falling birth rate and the rising divorce rate,' the study says.

> *'The next 20 years will see the rapid growth of beanpole families – long, thin family groups of three or four small generations'*

'Twenty years ago, family groups were "horizontally broad", comprising two or three generations with many children in each nuclear family. The next 20 years will see the rapid growth of beanpole families – long, thin family groups of three or four small generations.'

More than half of the adult population lives in 'beanpole' structures, the study says. With fewer brothers and sisters and cousins, children are growing up faster. 'Children are being starved of the companionship of family members of their own age. Individualism is of growing importance,' the study says.

'This could lead to greater social dislocation, with children growing up isolated from other children and younger adults. It could also encourage greater social isolation, with teenagers adopting a more selfish attitude towards life.'

Pressure on 40- to 60-year-olds is growing sharply. This 'sandwich generation' is caught between children, who need financial help, and elderly relatives, who need looking after.

The rising divorce rate, the study predicts, 'will make family structures more fluid and lead to a rise in "boomerang children" – children who leave the family home only to return at a later date after a marriage or long-term relationship breaks down'.

While the growth of the 'beanpole' family may promote more contact between different generations, Mintel says it will make it even harder for the middle-aged to strike a work/life balance.

This generation 'will feel that their quality of life is being reduced due to time pressures. The strain will be particularly acute for women, more and more of whom are working at senior levels but still carry out most of the caring responsibilities.'

> *'Children are being starved of the companionship of family members of their own age. Individualism is of growing importance'*

The rising divorce rate partly explains the growth of the 'beanpole' family. With almost one in two marriages ending in divorce, many adults have at least two families, each with a single child. While the number of married couples will fall over the next 10 years, the number of cohabiting couples – who have been married before – is set to double, the study says.

Medical advances, which mean the elderly live longer, explain why four-generation extended families are now the norm.

The Mintel study is backed by leading family researchers. Julia Brannen, professor of family sociology at the Institute of Education at London University, said: 'People are living longer, but family units are small and they are getting smaller and thinner all the time, just like a beanpole.

'Soon the issue will be: will young people miss the boat and not have families at all? We are already down to one child and soon for many people it may be none. Nuclear Family, RIP.'

■ This article first appeared in *The Observer*, 5 May 2002.

Births outside marriage rise to 40%

Fertility rates fall again as population fails to renew itself

Births outside marriage have increased over the past 10 years from 30% to 40% of all children born in England and Wales.

A majority of the babies born to women under 25 were born outside marriage last year. They accounted for 89% of births to teenagers and 63% of those to women aged 20-24.

The proportion fell to just over a third for women in their late 20s and about a quarter for women in their 30s, according to a report yesterday from the office for national statistics.

Birth statistics for 2001 recorded a continuing fall in fertility rates. There were 595,000 live births last year, compared with 604,000 in 2000.

The average for women in England and Wales is now 1.64 children, compared with a peak of 2.93 in 1964. This confirmed figures from the ONS in May suggesting that women were having fewer children than at any time since the government started keeping records of the nation's fertility in 1924.

The fertility rate is far below the average of 2.1 children per woman throughout her childbearing life, the rate that is needed for the population to replace itself in the long term without inward migration.

A new regional breakdown showed fertility rates varied from a low of 1.58 in north-east England to 1.74 in the West Midlands. Officials said the difference might be explained by ethnic factors showing lower fertility among the white population.

The average age of women at the birth of their first child increased from 25.7 in 1991 to 27.1 in 2001. In 2000, the under-18 conception rate in England and Wales was 43.8 per 1,000 women aged 15-17. This was 3% lower than in 1999. Just over half these teenage conceptions led to a birth.

By John Carvel, Social Affairs Editor

Highest teenage birth rates were in the north-east and Wales with 35.2 births per 1,000 women aged 15-19, compared with a low of 22.1 in the south-east.

Birth statistics for 2001 recorded a continuing fall in fertility rates. There were 595,000 live births last year, compared with 604,000 in 2000

In London, 32.5% of all conceptions were terminated by an abortion, compared with a low of 19.1% in the east.

- The ONS also published an ethnic profile of the UK. It said the minority ethnic population in 2001/2 was 7.6% of the total. The proportion varied from 9% in England to 2% in Scotland and Wales.
- Nearly half the UK total minority ethnic population lived in London, where they comprised 29% of all residents.

- Indians were the largest minority group in the UK, followed by Pakistanis, black Caribbeans, black Africans and those of mixed ethnic background.
- The mixed group had the youngest ages, with 55% under 16. The white group were the oldest, with 16% over 65.
- Bangladeshi men and women had the highest unemployment rates at 20% and 24% respectively. In 2001/2 40% of Bangladeshi men under 25 were unemployed, compared with 12% of young white men. Pakistani and Chinese groups were twice as likely as white or black people to be self-employed.
- Indian girls and boys in England and Wales were the most likely to get five or more GCSEs at grade C or above.
- In 2001/2 people from Chinese, Indian, black African and other Asian groups were more likely to have degrees than white people in the UK.
- After adjusting for age differences, Pakistani and Bangladeshi men and women were three to four times more likely than the general population to describe their health as bad in 1999. Indian men and women reported the most diabetes.
- In England in 1999, Bangladeshi men were the group most likely to smoke cigarettes (44%), followed by Irish (39%) and black Caribbean men (35%). More than 34% of Irish men drank over the recommended maximum 21 units of alcohol a week and almost a fifth of Irish women drank over the recommended 14 units. All other minority ethnic groups were less likely than the general population to drink above these levels.

Does Britain really like its children?

Jane Cunningham finds out

Many of you will have taken a holiday abroad in the last 12 months. Even after copious jugs of local brew, it probably won't have escaped your notice that children are, well, positively welcome there.

Our continental counterparts don't insist on an 8pm bedtime, when kids must be banished to their rooms while Mum and Dad go off to a restaurant or the cinema. They do the unthinkable – they take their kids with them and enjoy family time together.

Elena Solis, whose native country is Spain, has lived in London for 11 years and has two young children. She says: 'In the Mediterranean, families congregate in the squares all evening and while parents have coffee, the children play. Kids are more integrated into the process of going out – there is less of a distinction between adults' and children's lives.'

In hotels and restaurants, there is no surly maître d' glaring at the kids as though they're carrying a virulent form of the plague. More often than not, on the continent, the children have their hair ruffled kindly and a sugary lolly popped in their mouths, by way of a genuine 'pleased to see you' greeting. Could it happen here? Not unless we do something about our attitude problem.

Could do better

The National Family and Parenting Institute recently commissioned a study, *Is Britain Family-Friendly?* The report looks at issues such as support for paternal leave, childcare provision and flexible working arrangements – well-worn areas that traditionally fail to meet standards set by other countries – and the verdict reads like a poor school report. 'Could do better' sums up Britain's

RIGHT START
For your family

attitude to combining work and family responsibilities and putting children and families at the heart of all government policies.

The report looks at issues such as paternal leave, where Denmark leads the way, offering a standard paid 10 days compared with the UK, where there is no set provision. British men work the longest hours in Europe: on average 46 per week, against Belgium's average of 40.9 hours.

Working mums, too, are paying the price, and not only in terms of time. Childcare is a continual worry, with the needs of many UK working parents failing to be met by state or company nursery provision. As Matt Seaton, editor of the *Guardian*'s parenting section, points out, 'It's a fact that middle-class people pay more per hour to the person who digs

'I had to take my baby twins to hospital, where there were some very steep steps to negotiate with the double-buggy. On the way down, I slipped and the buggy fell forward, dropping the babies on the floor. No staff came rushing to help, even though the security guard could see me.'
Shelley Carter, Bristol

'I was happily breastfeeding my baby in a motorway service station restaurant when a member of staff asked if I would move to the toilet.'
Rebecca Haines, Renfrewshire

their garden than to the person who looks after their child. A priority for making Britain more family friendly would be a more comprehensive system of state-funded nurseries, as exists in France.'

Roads to nowhere

Traffic safety is one area where Britain does actually shine, according to the report, with one of the lowest levels of road-traffic deaths in Europe. But take a look at the situation for child pedestrians.

Every year in Britain over 130 children die and more than 4,500 are seriously injured while walking

or cycling – no wonder parents feel walking to school is an unsafe option. Meanwhile countries such as Sweden lead the way with cycle lanes, pedestrian-only roads in residential areas and restricting car priority. In other words, Swedish kids are leading the kind of lives we'd like our own to lead: more healthy and independent. They play outside, they enjoy a safer walking environment and they are able to cycle more freely.

Britain is toying with something called the home zone: a street or group of streets where pedestrians have priority and cars travel at little more than walking pace. A pilot programme of nine home zones has been established in Leeds, Manchester, Plymouth and other towns around the country, but you don't need to be Carol Vordermann to figure out that nine zones across the UK doesn't add up to much more than a token gesture.

Away-day disasters
Planning a day out with your children in this country can highlight other areas where Britain fails families miserably. First off, you'll pay more in London for a one-day travel card than any other city in Europe. Last year, a one-day travel card for London cost £3.90. In Rome, they paid £1.76, in Amsterdam, a respectable £2.06, and in Berlin, you can see the city for £2.47.

Our public transport comes in for a hammering, too. Germans enjoy low-level buses, capable of taking buggies unfolded, as standard, and while there are low-level buses in Britain, they are too few and infrequent to be a reliable source of transport for parents with young children. At the same time you can expect little or no help getting on and off public transport from paid transport employees, few lifts for easy access and nominal child discounts for attractions.

Try negotiating steep steps at the railway station with a buggy and three kids in tow, changing your baby's nappy on a toilet floor or being shunted into a grotty, damp room in the pub with all the ambience of a cemetery. It's a wonder we bother at all.

Thumbs up
To Costa Coffee shops for giving out free Baby Chinos (an espresso-size cup of frothy milk with a sprinkle of chocolate).

To the National Trust for providing over 1,000 children's events every year, and taking part in the National Family Weekend giving kids free entry to NT properties.

To Barclays Bank for re-organising their maternity leave arrangements, offering a return bonus equivalent to 12 weeks' pay and offering term-time contracts.

Thumbs down
To the Government for initiating 5 paid days a year for parents to care for unwell children, but only those born after 15 December 1999. Do they think older kids don't get ill?

To Starbucks Coffee shops for charging £1.25 for a kid's Hot Chocolate.

To Marks & Spencer for continuing to put sweets at most checkouts, even though they know mums don't like it.

Shopping blues
Parents are often advised simply to avoid supermarkets altogether rather than try to negotiate the wire trolleys, the lack of toilets and the sweets at the checkout with their tantruming toddlers. And if all that doesn't get you, then the tuts from pensioners or the smug glances from other mothers with quiet children will.

The truth is that being family friendly isn't just about practical issues. Just as important, it's about attitudes. Child psychologist Dorothy Einon says: 'In other parts of Europe, families do more things together, such as going out to eat. It is part of everyday life for them to have longer lunch breaks where the children join in. Shopping is often a more local event, where individuals and families are known, and therefore difficult behaviour is more likely to be tolerated.

'It's true to say that in Britain, the Victorian attitude about not showing our feelings in public persists, particularly among older generations, who feel that a child's

behaviour reflects upon the parents,' adds Dorothy Einon.

Building a better world
So what is being done to help families?
- The National Childcare Strategy is dedicated to increasing childcare provision
- Pressure groups are lobbying for more maternity benefits
- Flexible working patterns are being looked at by large companies
- Councils are recognising the importance of play areas
- John Lewis Stores have a particularly family-friendly environment: their new Solihull store was built from scratch using designers who are parents themselves. Hence, aisles are wide enough for two double buggies to pass comfortably!
- Buggy-friendly buses are finally being introduced in Britain
- Museums are targeting children with specific attractions. For example, London's British Museum hosts a range of family events, and has recently opened a centre for young visitors.

The Government is beginning to address family-friendly issues in an open and co-operative way, but paper-pushing consultation documents won't right the wrongs overnight.

What we as parents must take on board is a responsibility to challenge the traditional British view of children and families. We must earn respect for ourselves as parents and for our children. Lobby your council, complain about the bus-driver who wouldn't wait while you sorted out shopping, baby and buggy, start a summer playscheme, demand a clean and safe swimming pool – the list is a long one. Don't give up until we've created a world where our children's needs are heard and a safe, friendly environment is theirs by right.

- Reproduced by kind permission of *Right Start*, the family life magazine for parents of children aged 6 months to 7 years. Visit their web site at www.rightstartmagazine.co.uk

© *McMillan Scott plc 2001*

Families and work

Information from the National Family & Parenting Institute

What can busy parents do?

All families will go through many changes – when children start nursery, go to school, change to secondary school and become teenagers. All the excitement that new opportunities bring goes together with the upheaval of change and sometimes the sadness of leaving the past behind. Some families will have to cope with the unexpected – job changes, divorce or accidents. These tips are intended as handy reminders for your family growing up.

- Trust your own instincts about what is right for you and for your children – there is no one perfect way to be a parent, only what works for each family.
- Be realistic.
- Accept that over time things will change and what is right for you when your baby is six months old will not necessarily be right when your child is six years old and certainly not when they reach 16.
- Share your responsibilities with others and only do what needs doing now. The rest can wait. Remember that happy parents can make for happy children.
- Learn to say no – what suits you and your family may not fit in with other people and you can suggest alternatives.

- Keep talking even when the going gets tough.
- Remember that most working parents will be facing the same dilemmas as you.

Getting organised for work

- Be organised when you are working.
- Put out everything you will need for the morning the night before.
- Get up half an hour earlier and leave plenty of time for saying goodbye.
- Share the work.
- Give your children the chance to do as much as they can for themselves.
- If you have a long journey home at the end of the day with your child, try to find ways to unwind on the way – snacks, drinks, stories, just chatting – whatever suits your child.
- When you have time off together, relax and enjoy it.

Marion is married with two small children age 2 and 4 and three older children aged 25, 20 and 16. She is a relief support worker in sheltered accommodation.
'I work weekends and nights providing emergency cover. I put in between 70 and 170 hours a month. My husband looks after the children. I was a sewing machinist before I had children. I went back to college and then became a support worker. I enjoy my job, but I work more out of financial necessity at the moment. The children do cry when I leave. I talk to my four-year-old and explain that the money I earn will buy him a new bike, but I worry sometimes that I'm buying toys to compensate. I appreciate it when managers can be flexible. Once I took the baby along to work with a bucket of toys.'

Leaving your child in someone else's care

- Take as much time as you can after your baby is born. This is a special time and you may be quite tired and emotional for a while. And remember that it is quite normal for you and your child to miss each other when you go back to work.
- The best care comes from a few people who are sensitive to a child's needs and show a genuine interest as they grow up.
- When you first leave your child in someone else's care it can help to start with a few short sessions when you stay until your child feels comfortable.
- Be firm when you leave and always say goodbye – this will reassure your child that every-

TODAY'S PRESENTATION

– HOW DID YOU GET IN HERE?!

MUM!

Simon Kneebone

thing is fine. Try to set aside your own worries, however hard it may be.

■ Stick to a predictable routine so that your child knows what to expect, including special ways of saying goodbye that your child can join in with, for example always hug or use a special goodbye rhyme.

■ Talk to your child about leaving and coming back later. Even though younger children can't understand what you say, they can pick up your mood. If you are calm and relaxed, your child is more likely to follow your example.

■ Take along:
  – a familiar, favourite toy
  – a special cup and bowl
  – a special teddy bear or
  – a comfort blanket.

■ Give the carer information about routine, your child's likes and dislikes, medical information and emergency numbers. If possible, leave time to exchange information each day about how your child is getting on. Phone during the day or turn up unexpectedly occasionally if you need to reassure yourself that things are OK.

■ It can help your child if other children you already know go to the same childminder or nursery.

■ If you are concerned about anything, talk to the carer. If things don't improve, think about changing your childcare. By the same token, if your child is happy, remember to let the carer know that her efforts are appreciated.

Keeping in touch with older children

■ If you have teenagers, keep in touch by using mobile phones.
■ Always tell your children where you will be and how you can be contacted.

Making time for the children

■ Don't answer the phone for an hour in the evenings so that you have time to unwind or talk over the day.
■ Spend time with your children just doing whatever the children want to do.
■ Be a 'positive parent' – give your children lots of praise, be consistent, be firm about what is and is not allowed.

Pat is a freelance journalist with two children aged 15 and 17.
'My children take my work for granted. They are really very considerate when I occasionally say I can't give them a lift.

My husband tried as much as possible to work shifts that would enable him to be at home with the children and to help me. I would have liked to talk to more working mothers – I was desperate to share information and receive reassurance that I was not neglecting my children when I returned to work. But it's also true to say that no one had prepared me for the emotional roller-coaster that becoming a mother entailed. I was absolutely shredded when I returned to full-time employment. I missed the baby terribly – I would follow mothers with prams around Fleet Street at lunchtime just to get a "fix" of a baby! I also missed my older daughter's first steps – I still haven't forgiven myself. The nanny told me about it when I returned home in the evening.'

■ The above information is from *Families and Work*, a publication produced by the National Family & Parenting Institute. Visit their web site at www.nfpi.org for further information.

© *National Family & Parenting Institute*

Experiments in living

A new factsheet, *Experiments in Living: The Fatherless Family*, reviews the research findings into the effects of family breakdown, and finds that the decline of the two-parent, married-couple family has resulted in poverty, ill-health, educational failure, unhappiness, anti-social behaviour, isolation and social exclusion for thousands of women, men and children.

Lone mothers are poorer, more depressed and more unhealthy than mothers in two-parent families. Non-resident fathers have higher death rates, drink more heavily, and risk losing contact with their children.

But the heaviest costs of these 'experiments in living' fall on children. They are more likely to suffer deprivation and ill-heath; to be unpopular with other children and to be in trouble at school, to get excluded and leave school early; to suffer physical and sexual abuse, and to run away from home; to drink, smoke, take drugs, become young offenders, engage in early and unprotected sexual intercourse, contract sexually transmitted infections and become teenage parents.

As young adults, they are more likely to be unqualified, unemployed and poor; to be homeless, offending and to go to jail; to suffer from poor physical and psychological health; to form unstable relationships and to have children outside any partnership.

Nor are the costs of family breakdown confined to the mothers, fathers and children of these families. They are passed on to the rest of society through their association with increased crime and violence, a weakening of community ties and an increased dependence on state welfare.

Experiments in Living can be downloaded free from www.civitas.org.uk

■ The above information is from Civitas: the Institute for the Study of Civil Society's web site which can be found at www.civitas.org.uk

© *Civitas: the Institute for the Study of Civil Society*

How do fathers fit in?

Information from Civitas

There is a tendency today to speak of 'parents' or 'carers' rather than 'mothers' or 'fathers'. People often say that the most important thing in raising children is to give them lots of love, something that all parents can do, regardless of whether they are a mother or a father. However, there are also many ways that mothers and fathers can bring unique strengths to their relationships with their children. In real people's lives, you can see these contributions, and they have been measured by social scientists. Fathers – just like mothers – always matter.

Two heads are better than one

Richness of care

A child who has both a mother and a father benefits from an increased richness of care. In other words, children with both a mother and a father can benefit from more caring, as well as a variety of caring styles.

Bridges to the world

Through their fathers and mothers, children have access to a vast network including grandparents, cousins, aunts and uncles, friends of the family, work colleagues, community organisations, faith communities, and even personal histories. Fathers and mothers provide 'bridges' to all these aspects of the outside world, providing more experiences for children as well as practical opportunities such as job possibilities.

Mothers benefit from fathers' support

If a mother can count on her children's father to help with keeping the house clean and in good repair, caring for the children, paying the bills, and planning for the future, she probably will be a happier, more

> *Children with both a mother and a father can benefit from more caring, as well as a variety of caring styles*

effective parent. The support a mother receives from her child's father can even help her be more competent and sensitive when feeding her baby. Mothers seem to gain the most security when they are married and know the father is committed to a lifelong relationship to her and their child.

> *The important thing to remember is that mothers and fathers often bring different strengths and styles to their parenting roles*

Breadwinning

Today, most families rely upon the incomes of both mothers and fathers. However, fathers still provide the lion's share of income. Fathers are either the sole earners or the main earners in two-thirds of two-parent households. Moreover, fathers' earnings are uniquely linked to many positive results for children, even when mothers' earnings are taken into consideration.

Complementary roles

It often is useful, as well as accurate, to generalise about average differences between men and women. Whether these differences are due more to inborn biological chemistry, or social pressures, or some combination of the two, is much debated.

It is generally agreed that men and women should no longer be regarded as 'opposites'. The important thing to remember is that mothers and fathers often bring different strengths and styles to their parenting roles. These roles complement each other, meaning that they are not interchangeable and are each necessary for healthy childrearing.

© Civitas

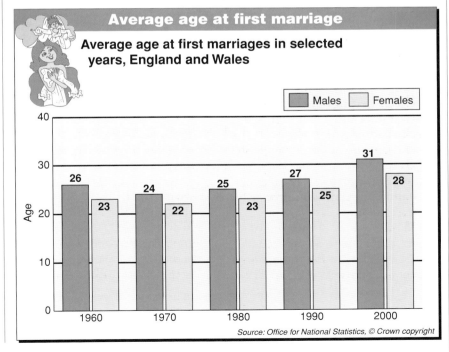

Average age at first marriage

Average age at first marriages in selected years, England and Wales

Source: Office for National Statistics, © Crown copyright

Stepfamilies

Challenges, myths and rewards. Information from Parentline Plus

A stepfamily is formed when a parent takes a new partner. In the past they were created as a result of the death of a parent. Now they are often formed after separation or divorce. They are sometimes called re-ordered or reconstituted families but stepfamilies are not the original family put back together again, they are a new group of people forming a new family and they can take a long time to stabilise – between two and ten years.

Questions and answers

How many people live in step-families?

Estimates vary, because they use different definitions of a stepfamily – most only count stepfamilies with dependent children living full-time in the household. Research shows that over 1 million dependent children live in full-time stepfamilies (GHS, 1991). However, most of these children have two households, so for every family with resident dependent stepchildren and every lone-parent family there is often at least one other family which is also a stepfamily. If we then add in children over 16, and not in full-time education, it is likely that as many as 18 million people in the UK are involved in stepfamily life.

What influences children's resilience to the impact of divorce and separation?

The most important factor is the parenting style. A firm but caring style – loving, clear, fair and consistent – provides vital support to children experiencing family change.

The presence of other reliable caring adults can also play a vital role in offsetting the impact of family disruption on a child. This could be a grandparent, family friend or professional e.g. a teacher or youth worker and, in time, a stepparent.

Being able to talk to other

Parentline plus

children can help. Children often want to compare their feelings about family change but they often feel isolated and alone. Adults can make a difference by creating opportunities for children to support each other.

. . . the challenges

What are the particular challenges for stepfamilies?

All family life is complicated but stepfamily life can be more so because of the variety of relationships and histories involved. It can be hard work:

- The emotional impact of separation, divorce or death has an effect on all members of a stepfamily and requires patience and understanding from adults who may feel very differently from children about the changes which have occurred.
- Problems from previous relationships may remain unresolved and may affect the way each member of the family feels about the new family. Difficulties over contact arrangements can also occur, so real diplomacy is needed to ensure that the children's needs are met.
- Finances can be very complicated. With child support going in and out of the family the finances of all the adults can have an instant impact on their own and other households. Legal issues e.g. parental responsibility, inheritance, custody are also complicated.
- Divided loyalties between adults and children, anxieties about favouritism, and feelings of rejection are common. Guilt is a feeling that can overwhelm adults and children.
- Different attitudes towards child-rearing and family life can lead to disagreements in stepfamilies.

New customs and routines have to be developed over time.

- Sex and sexuality can be a problem. Children are confronted with the idea of their parent as a sexual being which can feel very uncomfortable for them.
- Time is often an issue. Time is needed for the couple to be alone to strengthen their relationship – the key to the stepfamily's success. Time is also needed for stepparents to develop a relationship with stepchildren and for parents to be alone with their children to reassure them that their love for them has not changed.

How do the traditional pressure points of family life affect stepfamilies?

- Events which all families find difficult can be more stressful for stepfamilies. It takes time to build a new family.
- The arrival of a baby for the new couple can have an impact on the roles of all of the members of the stepfamily affecting stability.
- Coping with teenagers, and the challenges which they pose for parents, stepparents and others, can lead to difficulties – especially over discipline.
- Family obligations in caring for elderly or frail relatives can be particularly complicated for stepfamilies.
- The marriage of the new couple can cause problems. For the children it may finally confirm that their original family cannot be recreated. Stepfamily

All family life is complicated but stepfamily life can be more so because of the variety of relationships and histories involved

weddings also raise questions of who should be invited and what each person's role is.

- A death in a stepfamily can provoke different reactions, acting as a reminder of the different relationships in the extended family.

. . . the myths

Myths about stepfamilies affect people's attitudes and behaviour.

Wicked stepmothers?

Fairytales are full of wicked stepmothers, but no one is all bad, just as no one is all good. Being a stepmother is a very challenging task – partly because women tend to have such high expectations of themselves, partly because it is often expected that a woman can automatically care for children. Some stepmothers never expected to have children, and feel unsure about the basic rudiments of childcare.

Abusing stepfathers?

Stepfathers are often thought of as a potential risk to children, but the evidence does not support this. Many men enjoy the challenges of childrearing and become very supportive figures in their stepchildren's lives.

Happy families?

People often expect that things will be better the next time around. They may be, but it takes time and effort. It is not automatic.

Some stepfamilies try to act like a 'nuclear' family. But a stepfamily is not the same as a nuclear family, it is born of loss, the birth parent and children share a history of which the stepparent is not part and there is another birth parent outside the household.

Love conquers all?

Sometimes partners think that because they love each other so much, problems will be easy to deal with. They won't. Love is not enough. There has to be a real commitment from both adults to making the new family work for the children and the adults. The stepparent has to want to care for the children; has to learn to like and maybe even love them. The parent has to recognise that the stepparent needs time to do this and will never be the same as, or a replacement for, the birth parent, but instead an additional adult.

Instant brothers and sisters?

Children and adults often think that it will be fun to have step- and half-siblings. Some of the time it will be but this is not automatic. The children may not like each other. They may feel jealous of each other, and resentful of the additional demands for time and attention from their parent.

. . . the rewards

What do adults and children gain from living in a stepfamily?

- Working together to solve difficulties can be rewarding for all.

'It was really hard for everyone to start with, but now we've got past that there's a big sense of achievement. We're proud of the family we've made.'

- Children gain a wider family. Stepparents, stepgrandparents and stepsiblings can all provide additional friendship and support.

'One of the best things about having a stepmother is that you can talk to her about things that might be difficult to ask your mum. My stepmum isn't like a mum, we have a different kind of relationship. But she's someone really important who cares about me and my dad.'

- Positive adult role models and important life skills.
- The new couple provides a positive adult model for children.

'Mum looks really good these days. She used to cry and drink and be so awful. With Ted she laughs and is happy again.'

- Children often come through into adult life with a greater capacity to adapt. They can learn to be more tolerant and to compromise and can be enriched by experiencing and learning about different lifestyles first hand.

'When I first met Michael I didn't like him. But he treated me as his equal and I learned so much about life from him.'

- Stepfamilies can bring a sense of belonging and comfort to children.

'I used to feel a bit lonely sometimes when it was just me and Mum. Now it's fun 'cause there's lots going on. Also, I like it when Adam takes me and Sam to football and stays to watch us play. Mum's not very keen on football.'

- Stepfamilies are a reinvestment – they reveal how resourceful people can be on a daily basis when they are committed to building families in which everyone can flourish.
- Adults have the opportunity to learn from past mistakes and all family members can benefit from other lessons learned, that relationships need to be worked at, and that it is important to value those around you.

'I think families divorcing helps children quite a lot to understand a bit more about how really important it is to value your family and everything.'

Facts and figures

1 in 4 children has parents who get divorced. Over half their mothers and fathers will remarry or repartner forming a stepfamily.

1 in 2 of these stepfamilies will have a new child of the stepcouple. Around 2.5 million children live in stepfamilies.

- The above information is from Parentline Plus's web site: www.parentlineplus.org.uk

© Parentline Plus

Grannies and Gramps

Grandparenting

By Maire Ni Reagain

Missing my granny happens around certain foods. To this day I can't make bread-and-butter pudding without dissolving into the margarine. Even now, five years after she passed away, the smell of a really good stew is almost more than I can bear. Granny and my love for her become one with the memory of heaps of little thick pancakes drenched with honey, sherry trifles, and enormous plum puddings. The family feasts that happened only when my granny was around.

The whole granny extravaganza was enhanced by holidays in her huge, draughty (haunted?) house. Memories of late summer nights, both of us in the kitchen in the front of the fire, sucking boiled sweets, watching the post-watershed television that I wasn't allowed to at home because it gave me nightmares. I'd creep upstairs with the nightlight for the altar on the landing, my nights would be full of dreams stuffed with drama because of the television. I remember the long dark corridor to her room, the stiff key that wouldn't turn in her lock when the bogey man came to get me and I remember being revived in the morning by a breakfast table groaning with delights.

The world of granny was so different to the world of home and yet I felt completely part of it. It was full of different characters, different rules, different experiences and quite significantly a different pecking order. For a start, in this world my mother was not at the top of the heap. In my granny's world, granny ruled and there were no pretenders to the throne. Given that they were so hugely different in outlook and disposition, having this second matriarch in my life was a wonderful, balancing, life enhancing experience.

Why are grandparents so important?
The list of reasons why is endless.

For a start they provide a link with the child's family history. They are keys that can unlock secrets as to why parents are the way they are (good and bad). They can represent an oasis of peace for a child in an unhappy family and they can be a safe source of respite for parents. At best they can be childminders saving parents a fortune in childcare costs. When terrible problems strike they can be the soldiers that keep on marching when the first line of defence crumples. Grandparents when they are fighting for their grandchildren can be very courageous indeed. Some of the most proactive members of disabled children's internet newsgroups are grandparents, fuelled by love and not held back by the day-to-day exhaustion felt by the parents themselves.

Even where the family history is murky and where grandparents fulfil no apparently useful role (there are of course many abysmal grandparents in the same way as there are many abysmal parents) their sheer awfulness can provide family cohesion, uniting them against a common enemy.

Krystina Winters remembers family get togethers with their grandparents: 'They were from peasant stock and had grown up knowing real hunger. They used to slobber and burp and belch and really shovel their food down. My grandmother used to blow her nose in the linen table napkins when we were at restaurants. They also weren't very nice to my father and he used to get very despondent at their disapproval even though he was a really successful businessman and it was hard to imagine them ever inhabiting the same world. Dad used to become a despairing little boy around them. We really felt united when we were with them, both in wanting to protect him, and in our disgust at our grandparents generally. This kind of unity was otherwise uncharacteristic of our family as we were usually at loggerheads with each other!'

Grandparents at their best
Renee Nyman can tell you all about that. She was reared by her grandparents. Her mother was a woman full of conflict and anger and although she grew up with a room set aside for her in her mother's house Renee spent six out of seven nights in her grandparents' house. She felt especially close to her grandfather: 'My grandparents provided security, love and everything I wasn't getting at home. They were all that my parents should have been but weren't. It was my granddad that packed my school lunches, drove me to the childminder, took care of me and told me that he loved me. Although they weren't physically affectionate (neither was my mother) I was never in doubt that they loved me. On days that I stayed at my mother's, my grandfather used to ring me to make sure that I wanted to be there and tell me he was phoning because he missed me so much.

'I don't believe I lost out on anything being reared by my grandparents because my mother had nothing to give me. Even now she and I are like strangers when we're together. When my grandfather died I never knew grief like it. I miss him to this day.'

A second chance

Some grandparents see their relationship with their grandchildren as an opportunity to undo all the mistakes. Not everyone feels that they deserve the opportunity.

'They really bug me,' said one friend. 'My most significant childhood memories consist of dad's drunken episodes when he used to take his belt to me. Now he's like Father Christmas on the phone to my two boys ho-ho-ing away. He and my mum want more visits, more photographs, more involvement but the memories of the beatings and of mum's just pretending it wasn't happening, causes the bile to rise. I don't want to cut off contact because the kids get something out of it, but at some point I'm going to tell them about what went on so I suspect my mum and dad are living on borrowed time as far as their grandson's affections are concerned.'

Renee Nyman recognises that her relationship with her grandfather had something to do with second chances also. Before her mother was born her grandparents had a son who was killed in a tragic accident on their farm. Her grandfather always blamed himself. When her mother was born her grandparents were very strict and overprotective, something that Renee's mother found herself incapable of forgiving. After a few drinks Renee's mum would telephone and be abusive to Renee's grand-mother citing all the reasons for her resentment. Renee's relationship with her grandparents on the other hand was very relaxed and they 'spoilt her rotten'. They were liberal with

Some grandparents see their relationship with their grandchildren as an opportunity to undo all the mistakes

Having grandparents situated in comfortable surroundings and in a different environment to the one that the child usually lives in can enrich the child's life in every way

her and imposed none of the restrictions on her that they'd imposed on her mother.

Visits and holidays

Having grandparents situated in comfortable surroundings and in a different environment to the one that the child usually lives in can enrich the child's life in every way. Refreshing holidays which really revitalise involve a change in scene and the most common barriers to having holidays are financial ones. However, having a set of doting grandparents living beside the sea for example can mean the child can have a holiday away with minimal outlay.

'Provided you don't go to the well too often . . .' cautions another friend. 'There's a Chinese proverb that goes: "Fish and guests stink after three days."' In my experience, visits to grandparents are no different to staying with any other people. In fact it can be worse because there's often such a build-up. All that anticipation and high expectations of those chubby little faces exhibited in poloroid around the front room. But as soon as the nappies in the bathroom bin start to stink or little Charlie dries his hands in the curtains, then the bubble bursts.'

Fifteen-year-old Katie Jamieson sees things very differently. She's been visiting her granny in Anglesey, North Wales, since she was a baby. She and twins Oliver and Claire rarely visit for less than three weeks at a time and her granny is never bad tempered or makes them feel like they're imposing. In fact, 'my granny's always saying "Oh you should stay for longer" and she always looks like she really means it. I love visiting. For a start it's somewhere out of

London to go to, she lives right opposite the beach, she's a really great cook and she always arranges really good things for us to do and places to go to. She even welcomes my friends. We're quite close because I never feel I have to pretend because she knows me so well. I think she's excellent! Honestly, there's never been a day when she hasn't made me feel welcome.'

The ideal model

One thing I discovered when researching this piece is that everyone's thumbnail sketch of the ideal grandparent and the role that they should play is entirely different and also, that it is fluid. Sometimes for instance initial division could be overcome by a generous gesture on the part of the grandparent or parent. One parent said how she had been irritated by her husband's mother's invasion of her physical space. ('She just would stand too darn close.') It blinded her to the fact that this woman was a wonderful grand-mother. All this irritation dissolved when the grandmother really waded in to help out with the grandchildren when the mother developed a severe infection after the birth of her second child. 'Really I feel like such a cow when I look back on it. I was really unpleasant to Audrey just because she got on my nerves. I used to snipe about her to my own mother who herself, in the event, proved useless at my time of need. I think Audrey is the ideal grandmother now. If you'd asked me this time last year I blush to think what I might have said.'

Whatever the conflicting feelings of the adults, all the children that I talked to regarding their grandparents spoke of them with a great deal of love. Sadly sometimes for a generation to be happy it has to cut ties with the previous one and move on. Fortunately for most of us the little or big issues that we have are not so great that they have to come between our offspring and our parents, giving the chance for something very special to bloom.

■ The above information is from *Families* magazine's web site: www.familiesmagazine.co.uk

© Families

Double act

**What's it like to grow up the child of gay parents?
The young reporters of Children's Express find out**

Having two parents is great. So why should I be discriminated against because both my parents are women?' That's the view of 16-year-old Jessica from north London. She has lived with her two mums all her life. She's aware that her father lives in Ireland, but has never met him.

'I've always known my mum was gay,' she says. 'It was just something I accepted, like the fact that she has blonde hair or that she supports Arsenal.'

Yet Jessica felt that she had to keep the fact she has gay parents secret from everyone except a handful of friends. When people at school found out about her family background, she found herself the victim of bullying.

'My classmates discovered I had two mums when they came to parents' evenings together,' she says. 'The other kids were very cruel about it, calling me names and refusing to leave me alone. It made me feel like I didn't want to go to school any more. I had to fight back the tears because I wanted to appear brave; I dealt with the situation by bottling up my feelings.'

Jessica is one of thousands of young people up and down the country who live with gay parents: 'My best mates don't even know. They don't need to know. They're my friends, and stuff about my mum doesn't come into it, just like I wouldn't expect to know personal things about their parents.'

Howard Delmonte is a family and couples therapy coordinator at the Project for Advocacy, Counselling and Education (Pace), the only organisation in Britain offering support and advice for families with gay members: 'I think society struggles with the idea of gay men or lesbians having a child. But things are slowly changing.

'Our service aims to help parents to understand how best to support the child. We also help them appreciate what feelings the child will be going through.'

Jessica, though, isn't convinced that support groups offer any help to ordinary young people like herself: 'I really couldn't imagine ever wanting to go to one. They're just talk, and don't offer any real support.'

'For many young people, being part of a group can be incredibly supportive,' Delmonte insists. 'Peer support helps them realise they're not on their own and gets them to share their experiences with others.'

'I think society struggles with the idea of gay men or lesbians having a child. But things are slowly changing'

Unlike Jessica, many teenagers find their parents' sexuality tough to deal with. Liam is a 17-year-old student from north London. Last year, his mother announced that she was divorcing his father – and that she was a lesbian.

'We'd expected the divorce bit, so that wasn't too much of a surprise,' he says. 'But then the whole gay part really shocked us, especially my younger brother and sister.'

At first, Liam couldn't bring himself to tell anyone the news, but recently he's plucked up the courage to talk to his closest friends: 'I've been very careful who I've told. I've made sure the people I talk to would understand rather than fly off the handle. I hate the way that gay is used as a derogatory term.'

Liam's family shake-up has been an important learning experience for him. It's made him realise that not everything in life is straightforward: 'My friends, perhaps, don't confide in me so much now because they think I've got greater problems than them. They see my experience as a really negative thing, whereas I now see it as being mostly positive.'

■ Names have been changed. This article was written by Jenny Roe-Stanton, 16, Alisha Fuller, 16, Gabriella Gay, 15, Annabel Mcleod, 15, Akosua Bonsu, 15 and Ella Parry-Davis, 12. Children's Express is a programme of learning through journalism for young people aged 8 to 18; see www.childrens-express.org This article first appeared in the *Guardian*.   © *Children's Express*

Being a parent today

Information from Familyonwards

By Jill Curtis

I wonder if each generation believes that it is more difficult to be a parent today than it was in the 'good old days'. Whilst our grandparents tell us about how hard it was to be a parent during world war two, and our parents tell us of the difficulties of being a parent when there was long hair and Woodstock, today's parents find themselves coping with adolescents through a minefield of sex, drugs and family break-up.

Of course this generation of adolescents didn't invent sex, whatever they like to think. But the rules are not the same as they once were, and each set of children and their parents have to reassess the situation and come to some agreement about where they draw the line. It is easy to say 'that wouldn't have happened in my day' or 'I would never have dared go out dressed like that' but again each generation has to struggle for an identity and to shock the older generation. What about the Charleston? Spit curls and short skirts? Didn't they all shock in their time? Are they so very different from hot pants, mini skirts and torn jeans kept together by safety pins?

Children may look more mature, but the 15-year-old going-on-27 still needs a great deal of support and input from his or her parents

It is not easy to be a parent, it never was and never will be. But it is not easy being an adolescent either. We all hear about greater expectations upon the young today, and certainly looking at the number of kids who drop out of education, and even leave home, shows us that

something is very wrong somewhere along the line. Peer pressure from other children means that from an early age they are nudged into a way of behaving which is often way above what they can cope with emotionally. 'Keeping up' with the latest fashion, whether clothes, sex or drugs, becomes a very heavy burden indeed. Perhaps an even heavier one if trying to say 'no'. Children may look more mature, but the 15-year-old going-on-27 still needs a great deal of support and input from his or her parents. Eating disorders are rampant, in boys as well as girls, and so is adolescent depression. Sadly these two major illnesses can go unnoticed and untreated.

Children are expected to cope with the break-up of a family. Adults quite often will convince themselves that the children are not harmed by divorce, but that is not true, and is more about protecting the parents from recognising the distress in their children. Even if a couple divorces, they are not divorcing the children, and need to come together at times to continue being parents.

So whether you are a new parent, or a seasoned one, each step along the way brings with it joys and anxieties about doing the right thing for your child. When pacing the floor in the small hours with a crying baby, or pacing the floor because your daughter hasn't come home when expected, it all adds up to the same thing, parenting is a tough business and goes on for years. In one way, the little boy or girl grows up in a flash, and perhaps that is one reason grandparents love to be involved with the younger generation. They know how quickly it all goes by, and what an important job 'bringing up baby' is. Lucky are the parents today who can search the web and communicate with other parents who are concerned about the same issues. There is always someone to give suggestions and advice, and no one should even hold back from asking. Parenting goes on way past the nursery days, so enjoy the good times, and brace yourself for the hard times because that is what parenting is all about

■ The above information is from Familyonwards' web site which can be found at www.familyonwards.com

© Jill Curtis 2003

Listening to parents

Their worries, their solutions

Parents worry. They worry whether they are doing a good, or good enough job, and they worry about what kind of world their children will grow up in. They worry about things within their control, and outside their control. As this survey shows, they worry about just about everything – but a balance must be struck. We are in danger of becoming a nation of over-anxious parents who have forgotten how to trust our judgement.

The survey was conducted against the background of continuing public debate about parenting and family life.

The key findings

- Parents' biggest anxiety about family life in Britain is about the risks from drugs and alcohol. This was consistent across men and women, race, and social class, but showed variations in different parts of the country.
- Education is a major concern, particularly to parents living in London and East England.
- Parents found teenage years the most difficult to handle, but less than half wanted more information to help them through those years.
- Parents' recipe for a successful family life was spending time together and talking with each other – partners as well as children.
- Some parents value and want information about parenting and children, but a substantial number (48%) said they do not require more information about child development.
- Parents are most likely to seek information first from family and friends and then from local services, like their doctor, local school or playgroup.
- Other sources, including Government sources of information, were less popular.

- The Office of National Statistics published figures showing families are getting smaller, with an average of just 1.66 children per family. There were a spate of articles in the press on the benefits and problems of only children, and questions about why people were having fewer children.
- The average age of a mother giving birth for the first time is now 29.
- Recent figures show a drop in the divorce rate but the UK still topped the European divorce table. The drop coincided with a drop in the numbers getting married.
- New research looked at how parental conflict affects children and concluded that how parents argue, rather than whether children are present or absent, is what matters.
- Women with a dependent child are working 2.5 hours more a week relative to women without

We are in danger of becoming a nation of over-anxious parents who have forgotten how to trust our judgement

children, than they were during the early 1990s. However, they still work fewer hours than women without children.
- Parents do more in a day than 40 years ago. Research has found that they now do 8.4 activities a day compared with 7.2 in 1961, but less than one in ten parents said they had time to relax.
- Working mothers could affect their children's A-level results, according to research published by the Institute for Social and Economic Research. At the same time, a survey by a women's magazine found that 95% of working mothers frequently felt stressed, and 78% said they 'would quit their current job tomorrow given the chance'.

Who was surveyed?

Between 26 and 30 July 2001, 1,391 parents were interviewed in Great Britain. The survey was based on a representative sample of the population, and a booster survey with black and minority ethnic parents was also conducted.

- The above information is from the National Family and Parenting Institute's web site which can be found at www.nfpi.org

Stressed parents

Stressed parents 'failing'; teenagers pine for job-driven parents

*By Ben Summerskill and
Ginanne Brownell*

Millions of teenagers want to see more, not less, of their parents. One in five young people says British parents – who have some of the longest working hours in Europe – are too stressed to make time for them, according to a major nationwide study. More than half of all teenage boys wish their parents took more interest in their education.

'We were shocked to find so many children not sharing worries with their parents because they thought them too stressed,' said Adrienne Katz of Young Voice, who surveyed 2,200 children aged between 11 and 18. 'There is evidently a huge gap in communication between parents and teenagers which widens with age. Parents are just not aware of the pressure that teenagers are under in a society which is more and more driven by success.'

Fewer than half of Britain's 16-year-olds think their parents are 'helpful' with the issues they face as they grow up. Educational choices, how to handle money and sexual health are among problems that overworked parents don't have time to discuss.

'It's not neglect,' says 17-year-old Tony Hasnath from Brighton. 'Parents want the best for their children, but in today's world everything is complex and busy and there's no time. People need time to sit down and talk to their children. Parents are far too busy to take enough care and notice.

'Sometimes our parents think we've grown up independently and they think it's good that we mature on our own. But you do need guidance and support.'

The desire among teenage boys for parents to take an interest in their schoolwork comes as they fall behind girls in academic performance. Last year, for the first time, girls achieved better A-level results than boys. Boys have fallen behind girls at GCSE for the last two years. Of the teenage girls surveyed, 28 per cent also want parents to take more interest in their academic activities.

Two in five 16-year-olds feel 'worried' about the choices they have to make for the future. 'My father wanted me to become an imam or something like that,' said Tony Hasnath. 'I've decided I want to be an actor.'

> **'There is evidently a huge gap in communication between parents and teenagers which widens with age'**

A report from Daycare Trust, a childcare charity, confirmed last year that 61 per cent of working families now have parents away from home during early mornings, evenings, nights and weekends; 34 per cent have a parent working at weekends. The number is expected to double by 2007.

> **'It would be good to have more time together, but I understand they have to work. Sometimes you want to chat things through'**

The problem has worsened with the explosion in the number of call centres, shops and new technology businesses operating around the clock. 'I see my mum and dad for long periods only at the weekend,' said Tim Heath, 15, from Nottingham, whose parents work in a sixth-form college. 'It would be good to have more time together, but I understand they have to work. Sometimes you want to chat things through. You can do that with friends, but they don't always tell it to you straight. I don't always believe things people tell me at school about sex, for example.'

The survey also found that one in ten youngsters complained of parents who 'care too much'. 'You have to be wary of imposing on your kids your own dreams for success,' said Katz. 'There's substantial evidence that we're putting too much stress on young people. Parents who may be frustrated in their own careers should not compensate by trying to live their own dreams through their children.'

■ This article first appeared in *The Observer*, 21 April 2002.

Nine steps to more effective parenting

Raising children is one of the toughest and most fulfilling jobs in the world – and the one for which you may feel the least prepared. Here are some ways to tackle your child-rearing responsibilities that will help you feel more fulfilled as a parent, and enjoy your children more, too.

1. Nurture your child's self-esteem

Children start developing their sense of self as babies when they see themselves through your eyes. Your tone of voice, your body language, and your every expression are absorbed by your child. Your words and actions as parents affect your child's developing self-image more than anything else in his world. Consequently, praising your child for his accomplishments, however small, will make him feel proud; letting him do things for himself will make him feel capable and independent. By contrast, belittling your child or comparing him unfavourably to another child will make him feel worthless.

Avoid making loaded statements or using words as weapons: 'What a stupid thing to do!' or 'You act more like a baby than your little brother!' Comments like these bruise the inside of a child as much as blows would the outside. Choose your words carefully and be compassionate. Let your child know that everyone makes mistakes and that you still love him, even when you don't love his behaviour.

Your words and actions as parents affect your child's developing self-image more than anything else in his world

---

2. Catch your child being good

Have you ever stopped to think about how many times you react negatively to your child in a given day? You may find that you are criticising far more than you are complimenting. How would you feel about a boss who treated you with that much negative guidance, even if well-intentioned?

The more effective approach is to catch your child doing something right: 'You made your bed without being asked – that's terrific!' or 'I was watching you play with your sister and you were very patient.' These statements will do more to encourage good behaviour over the long run than repeated scoldings. Make a point of finding something to praise every day. Be generous with rewards – your love, hugs, and compliments can work wonders and are often reward enough. Soon you will find you are 'growing' more of the behaviour you would like to see.

3. Set limits and be consistent with your discipline

Discipline is necessary in every household. The goal of discipline is to help children choose acceptable behaviours and learn self-control. Children may test the limits you establish for them, but they need those limits to grow into responsible adults. Establishing house rules will help children understand your expectations and develop self-control. Some house rules might include: no TV until homework is done, and no hitting, name-calling, or hurtful teasing is allowed.

You may want to have a system in place: one warning, followed by consequences such as a 'time out' or loss of privileges. A common mistake parents make is failure to follow through with consequences when rules are broken. You can't discipline a child for talking back one day, and ignore it the next. Being consistent teaches your child what you expect.

4. Make time for your children

With so many demands on your time, it's often difficult for parents and children to get together for a family meal, let alone spend some quality time together. But there is probably nothing your child would like more. Get up 10 minutes earlier in the morning so you can eat breakfast with your child, or leave the dishes in the sink and take a walk after dinner. Children who are not getting the attention they want from their parents often act up or misbehave because they are assured of being noticed that way.

Many parents find it mutually rewarding to have prescheduled time with their child on a regular basis. For instance, tell your child that Tuesday is his special night with Mommy, and let him help decide how you will spend your time together. Look for other ways to connect with your child – put a note or something special in his lunchbox.

Adolescents seem to need less undivided attention from their parents than younger children. Because there are fewer windows of opportunity for parents and teens to get together, parents should do their best to be available when their teen does express a desire to talk or participate in family activities. Attending concerts, games, and other events with him communicates caring and lets you get to know about him and his friends in important ways.

Don't feel guilty if you're a working parent. It is the many little things you do with your child – making popcorn, playing cards, window shopping – that he will remember.

5. Be a good role model

Young children learn a great deal about how to act by watching you. The younger they are, the more cues they take from you. Before you lash out or blow your top in front of your child, think about this: is that how you want him to behave when he's angry? Be constantly aware that you are being observed by your children. Studies have shown that children who hit usually have a role model for aggression at home.

Model the traits you wish to cultivate in your child: respect, friendliness, honesty, kindness, tolerance. Exhibit unselfish behaviour. Do things for other people without expecting a reward. Express thanks and offer compliments. Above all, treat your children the way you expect other people to treat you.

6. Make communication a priority

You can't expect children to do everything simply because you, as parent, 'say so'. Children want and deserve explanations as much as adults do. If we don't take time to explain, children will begin to wonder about our values and motives and whether they have any basis. Parents who reason with their children allow them to understand and learn in a non-judgemental way.

> Model the traits
> you wish to cultivate
> in your child: respect,
> friendliness, honesty,
> kindness, tolerance

Make your expectations clear. If there is a problem, describe it to your older child, express your feelings about it, and invite your child to work on a solution with you. Be sure to include consequences. Make suggestions and offer choices. Be open to your child's suggestions as well. Negotiate with him. Children who participate in decisions are more motivated to carry them out.

7. Be flexible and willing to adjust your parenting style

If you frequently feel 'let down' by your child's behaviour, it may be because you have unrealistic expectations for him. Parents who think in 'shoulds' (for example, 'He

should be potty-trained by now') may find it helpful to do more reading on the matter or talk to other parents or child development specialists.

Your child's environment has an impact on his behaviour, and you may be able to modify his behaviour by changing his environment. If you find yourself constantly saying 'No' to your 2-year-old, look for ways to restructure his surroundings so that fewer things are off-limits. This will cause less frustration for both of you.

As your child changes, you will gradually have to change your parenting style. Chances are, what works with your child now won't work as well in a year or two.

Teenagers tend to look less to their parents and more to their peers for role models. Continue to provide guidance, encouragement, and appropriate discipline while allowing your child to earn more independence. And seize every available moment to make a connection!

8. Show that your love is unconditional

As a parent, you are responsible for correcting and guiding your child. But how you express your corrective guidance makes all the difference in how your child receives it. When you have to confront your child, avoid blaming, criticising, or fault-finding, which undermine self-esteem and can lead to resentment. Instead, strive to nurture and encourage even when you are disciplining your child. Make sure

> Because there are fewer windows of opportunity for parents and teens to get together, parents should do their best to be available when their teen does express a desire to talk or participate in family activities

he knows that although you want and expect him to do better next time, you love him no matter what.

9. Be aware of your own needs and limitations as a parent

Face it – you are an imperfect parent. You have strengths and weaknesses as a family leader. Recognise your abilities – 'I am loving and dedicated.' Vow to work on your weaknesses – 'I need to be more consistent with discipline.' Try to have realistic expectations for yourself, your spouse, and your children. You don't have to have all the answers – be forgiving of yourself. And try to make parenting a manageable job. Focus on the areas that need the most attention rather than trying to address everything all at once. Admit it when you're burned out. Take time out from parenting to do things that will make you happy as a person (or as a couple). Focusing on your needs does not make you selfish. It simply means you care about your own well-being, which is another important value to model for your children.

Note: All information on KidsHealth is for educational purposes only. For specific medical advice, diagnoses, and treatment, consult your doctor.

■ This information was provided by KidsHealth, one of the largest resources online for medically reviewed health information written for parents, kids and teens. For more articles like this one, visit www.KidsHealth.org or www.TeensHealth.org

© *KidsHealth*

Get with the programme

Parenting classes are suddenly big business. But are they all they're cracked up to be? Joanna Moorhead reports

Parenting courses are to the noughties what therapy was to the nineties: we're all flocking for our fix. Anywhere parents are to be found, from dinner parties to playgrounds, you will encounter the evangelists who say their lives have been changed for ever by seven evenings spent listening to a guru. Possibly not since the 1930s has adult education seemed so sexy.

Even the fact that you may so far have bucked the trend and avoided signing up for parenting classes does not mean you will be able to escape them indefinitely. Such courses are now deemed so useful that they are becoming de rigueur: it was reported this week that the parliamentary subcommittee reviewing the Children Act is likely to recommend that estranged couples who are warring over children should be obliged to take parenting classes to help resolve issues of contact and custody. Since June last year, magistrates have had the power to issue orders demanding attendance at classes for parents who have a child in trouble with the law. And earlier this year, David Blunkett (in his capacity then as education secretary) promised the same fate for parents who failed to deal with 'problem children' in school, or who were abusive towards teachers themselves.

According to Debbie Cowley of the Parenting Education and Support

---

Anywhere parents are to be found, from dinner parties to playgrounds, you will encounter the evangelists who say their lives have been changed for ever by seven evenings spent listening to a guru

---

Forum, an umbrella support group for parenting course-providers, there is (unpublished) evidence that around 25% of parents say they would participate if offered a place on a course.

'It gives you confidence; it gives you ideas; it gives you a sounding-board,' says Jennifer Velaise, mother of three boys, aged eight, five and two. 'I felt I had so many issues to deal with, and I wasn't sure I was going about anything in the right way.' Going on a parenting course one morning a week for five weeks hasn't made everything in the garden rosy, but it has made life a lot better for Velaise. 'It has helped that I was able to put things into a wider context, and also that my course was led by a psychotherapist who was able to talk quite specifically about individual problems. On issues like discipline, you were given tools to help you be a lot more effective. For example, I was always using the same punishment which was withdrawing the use of the video player; what I learned on the course was that it's far better to link the punishment to the crime. So, for example, if your child breaks a lamp and it was a deliberate

act and merits a punishment, that should be something like docking their pocket money to buy a new one.'

Expert input, though, is only one of the elements in most parenting courses. Group sharing, which, in practice, means finding out you're not the only one with worries or problems, is also a big part of the philosophy.

'Another thing that has helped is the idea of weekly family conferences,' says Jennifer. 'The two-year-old is too little, so during his nap we have a chat and each person gets time to talk about how the week has gone and so on. It brings up issues that seem quite funny but are real to them – for example, my five-year-old said recently he felt he wasn't being given enough trips to the park. We could see his point of view on that, so we're trying harder to give him more opportunities to play there.'

The course attended by Jennifer Velaise was run by an independent company named JoeyCo and cost £180. But as demand is still growing in this burgeoning sector, so too is the choice. If you're on a tight budget, you could take a class run by the charity Parentline Plus, one of the biggest providers of the 1,000 or so courses in the UK. Their parenting education comes free – and with a crèche.

Yasmin Allen, a single parent with children aged 15 and five, did a Parentline Plus course three years ago and feels it's made a huge difference, especially to her relationship with her eldest child. 'Having a teenager can seem so difficult – you feel you're lurching from one confrontational situation to the next,' she says. 'At first, I resisted the idea of going on a course, but things were going so badly I knew I had to do something. And the great thing about it was that, though many of the mothers I met had a lot more money than me, and many were in two-parent families, their problems were the same as mine.'

Parenting courses can also hint at what lies ahead for families. Helen Carruthers, mother of 10-year-old Rachel, eight-year-old John and five-year-old Benjamin, followed an eight-week video-based course put together by an Anglican charity called Care for the Family. 'It was helpful because it looked towards the next stage of parenting as well as the stage we were at,' she says. 'For example, we discussed issues around drug use in adolescence – and it's much better to have considered your feelings on this before you have to deal with it in reality.'

At the moment, it is mums rather than dads who make up the lion's share of participants on parenting courses – a fact that reflects time-flexibility rather than enthusiasm. Jennifer Velaise says that now her husband has seen how positive her experience was, he has signed up for a JoeyCo course too. Another parenting course-provider, the Parent Company, says that while the ratio of men to women on courses is something in the region of one in four, that rises to two in three for classes on raising boys – which is also its most popular class.

At the moment, it is mums rather than dads who make up the lion's share of participants on parenting courses – a fact that reflects time-flexibility rather than enthusiasm

---

The Parent Company differs from many other parent course-providers in that it offers specific two-and-a-half-hour themed seminars: you pick out the issue or issues that affect your family. Kerri Summers, mother of two young boys and one of the founders of the four-year-old company, says she used the model of corporate courses from her background with American Airlines, and applied it to time-starved parents looking for advice on how to raise their children.

'Our starting-point was that, in our corporate lives, when we needed to learn something fast, we went on a course where people who'd read all the books and knew all the arguments distilled their knowledge and made it interesting and useful to us in a few hours,' she says. 'So we took the same approach and made it work for parents who don't have the time to read loads of books or go on seven- or eight-week courses.'

'Vision-building', 'self-talk' and 'emotional conditioning' sound like buzz-words better suited to the boardroom than the dining-room table, and some may find this spillover of corporate jargon into a family setting rebarbative. One course-provider tells of a conference she attended where a speaker said that if she heard the phrase 'managing behaviour' one more time, she'd scream. In general, says Debbie Cowley of the Parenting Education and Support Forum, courses tend to be of two types: the prescriptive, which tells parents how they should handle particular situations, or the shared-experience model, which concentrates on building and changing relationships. The evidence suggests that it is the latter, rather than the former, that is most likely to succeed.

Whether parenting education proves effective in the long run remains to be seen. What is certain is that the idea we all grew up with – that parenting is basically commonsense, something you pick up on the job – looks increasingly outmoded. Pass the prospectus, will you?

© *Guardian Newspapers Limited 2002*

ER... HOW DO I FIT IN TO THE **PRODUCT HANDLING MANAGEMENT SYSTEM**?

– DON'T TRY, ITS THE NAPPY BUCKET...

SIMON KNEEBONE

A father writes: parenting

Room service? They can think again

By Tom Kemp

I wish that the childrearing experts would make up their minds. Most have told us that, if we want teenagers to mature into happy and successful adults, we should give them the independence they crave.

I have never found much difficulty in following this advice – not so much because I am anxious to do the right thing, as because I am bone idle. When the 16-year-old asks if he can go into town to see his mates, I almost always grunt 'I suppose so', simply because I can't face the row that would follow if I dared to say no.

Sometimes, I feel that I am far too lax. The other evening he asked if he could stay the night at Nick's house, and I said yes. It was only after he had disappeared down the road that it occurred to me that I hadn't a clue who Nick was or where he lived.

My wife hadn't heard of him, either. What would I tell the police if my boy failed to reappear the next day? 'He stayed the night with a friend, officer.'

'And which friend would that be, sir?'

'He's called Nick. Or maybe he's a she. I'm afraid that's all I know.'

'Very good, sir. We'll interview every Nicholas, Nikolai, Nicole, Nicola and Nicolette in London, and maybe we'll track him down.'

Some father I'd look. But then I tell myself that he always does reappear, and that at 16, he is allowed by law to leave home anyway. And what about all those experts who tell us that we must allow our teenagers to go their own way?

But now along comes Terri Apter, a psychologist and senior lecturer at Cambridge University, with a theory that every other expert has been talking rubbish. She told the conference of the National Family and Parenting Institute that the best thing that we parents can do for our teenagers is to mollycoddle them until they are well into their twenties.

Young people, she said, benefited from continued parental nurturing even after they had left the nest. Those given their independence suffered terribly, because they had unrealistic expectations of what they could achieve on their own.

So the one thing that I thought I was doing right turns out to be yet another thing that I am doing wrong.

I suppose that I should either have forbidden my boy to stay at Nick's, or, at the very least, I should have packed an overnight bag for him, driven him round to Nick's house, satisfied myself that Nick was a suitable friend and that proper arrangements had been made for my little treasure's stay, and told the boy loudly in the presence of his friend, as I kissed him goodbye, that he must remember to brush his teeth and to put on clean pants in the morning.

> When the 16-year-old asks if he can go into town to see his mates, I almost always grunt 'I suppose so', simply because I can't face the row that would follow if I dared to say no

I have a feeling that he would not have thanked me for that.

But the awful thing is that Dr Apter may have a point. When I think of my own circle of friends, the two most successful also happen to be the two most mothered people I know.

One is an immensely distinguished psychiatrist. I will always remember his mother telling him, in my presence, when he was in his late twenties and already a professor, that on no account should he buy a house without a separate dining room. 'You will never win the Nobel Prize, darling, if your guests have to eat in the kitchen.'

The other is a self-made multi-millionaire, who told me that, when he was 17, his mother used to bring him breakfast in bed when he was tucked up with his girlfriend. If my boys expect the same service, they can think again.

But then, my successful friends may be exceptions to the rule. Dr Apter may be quite wrong about the wisdom of mollycoddling our teenagers, and all the other experts may be right.

When I am asked to address the National Family and Parenting Institute, I shall say that parents should bring up our children however the hell we like. Whatever we do, we are bound to be wrong.

© *Telegraph Group Limited, London 2003*

Dads rule OK

By Maire Ni Reagain

Fantastic fathers

It is neither fashionable nor profitable to rave about our men folk, and it is infinitely more fun to write about their follies and foibles. However, although I would not generally describe myself as a lucky person I am fortunate in inheriting one great legacy: in common with all the women in the last four generations of my mother's line, my father and I have a wonderful affinity. I have no idea if this is nurture, nature, or just a fluke, but what I can say is that having such a good relationship caused my own expectations to be high. Consequently my daughters have a devoted father who has given up everything in terms of personal ambition for their sakes, and is now a full-time stay-at-home dad managing the paperwork for our autistic daughter's educational programme and looking after the baby.

Feeling irritated

While I am very appreciative, it doesn't stop me feeling irritated by the sainthood bestowed on him by outsiders, coupled with the whiff of disapproval of my apparent abandonment of the traditional female role. I'm not alone. A woman whose daughter was born with a severe facial disfigurement told me how a number of otherwise sane, down-to-earth women (and not just of the older generation either) said how she should count herself lucky to have a man like her husband. 'I was told that there was many a man who wouldn't be seen for dust if they found themselves in that situation. In the end I used to say "Well excuse me! I'll stop pulling out my hair and start digging deep in my bag for that gold medal instead . . ."' The praise is a backhanded criticism. The implication is that all men are selfish and uncaring, thus condemning all men for the sins of some. (It is also a gross oversimplification of what happens to families when crises hit the home.)

> Who better than a dad to introduce the topic of dads? Graham McGuiness is the father of two daughters, aged 5 & 7: 'Fathers so often are forgotten in the daily discussion and grind of family life, but are such an integral part of the family itself. Perhaps it is work or travel that keeps them at a distance, but experience proves that in some situations only Daddy will do. There are things my own children will speak only to their father about, and certainly fathers, we forget they do actually acquire some wisdom in their profession as a parent, even when they make as big a mess as the children. And mostly, we forget to listen.'

This impression is accentuated by the media who love to make a song and a dance about every icky-picky little effort made by men. For instance it made the news when Suma Chakrabarti took over the Department of International Development in Whitehall. This was not so much because he was the first Asian to be appointed to such a senior position but because he'd cut a deal with Government minister Claire Short which allowed him to spend more time with his six-year-old daughter. Consequently he starts work not before 9.30am (so he can breakfast with his daughter) and leaves work at 5.30pm in order that he can bathe her and read her a bedtime story. Needless to remark, if he'd been a woman no one would have batted an eye. Although this sort of reporting is irritating and

> 'Fathers so often are forgotten in the daily discussion and grind of family life, but are such an integral part of the family itself'

illustrates the deeply rooted sexism in society, it also illustrates that gradually attitudes are shifting.

The trouble with statistics . . .

Look on the internet under 'Fatherhood' and you'll be overwhelmed by sites chock-a-block with stern statistics proving how a family without a father is basically doomed. A friend of mine, a truly fantastic single mother, says that she thanks her lucky stars every day that her own highly disapproving mother hasn't access to the internet. As it is, 'Granny' terminates every argument with the words 'Stickstistics prove that . . . ' These sites would furnish her with a whole new set of 'stick-stistics' with which to browbeat her daughter.

One of the reasons this research is so pointless is that it misses the point. Sure, governments can produce damning statistics on how it affects children to be born into homes without fathers. These are irrelevant if you don't tackle the huge social and economic problems that result in young girls being so uninspired by their future prospects that changing dirty nappies seems like a fun option, and young men thinking that they have nothing to lose by having unprotected sex. There was a study of teenage mothers in inner-city Baltimore: one-third of their daughters also became teenage mothers, said the report. However, the authors noted, not one daughter or son who had a good relationship with his or her biological father had a baby before the age of nineteen. The conclusion: good relationships with fathers not only prevented daughters from becoming pregnant, but also prevented sons from creating pregnancies prematurely.

In theory . . .

Let's look more closely at this: I know of two cases where pregnancy was 'created prematurely' and yes indeed, the girls did have very bad relationships with their fathers. So the above theory is shown to be correct. However . . . these girls were impregnated by boys, who came from families where the fathers had great relationships with their sons. So the same theory is shown to be incorrect! To quote the immortal words of a very famous father, 'Do'h!'

I know, too, many fantastic single mothers and a sufficient number of deadbeat dads to be of the opinion that any dad is better than no dad. Not everyone is of that opinion. A friend has painful childhood memories of her own mother's desperation to have a father in her children's lives. She had to endure a succession of 'fathers' as mommy ricocheted between a succession of loser men. 'For Mom it was a case of any pop in a storm,' she quipped.

Joking aside . . .

The only reason that such statistics are useful (however flawed), is that they illustrate the point that a father's importance does not begin and end with the opening and closing of his wallet. It stands to reason that if a girl has a great father-daughter relationship, she doesn't have to go to bed with a man to experience male approval. Speaking personally, my father made me feel special and worthwhile, and that definitely fed a need in me. Fear of losing his approval caused me to restrain my behaviour. If that check hadn't been in place I might have made very different lifestyle choices. Enough of the praise already!

Even the best aren't perfect

The following are a few common complaints about dads:

- They are useless at multitasking. They'll feed the kids or dress them or take them out. They generally can't manage to combine even two out of three.
- They dress 'em strange. One mother who job shares with her husband told me: 'There have been days when my husband collects me from work and I am actually afraid to look in the back of the car for fear of what I'm going to see. Once Samantha aged four was dressed in a pair of fleecy leggings that are a tight fit on eight-month-old Alison. She was wearing them as shorts, over a swimming costume, and topped with a knotted hanky.'
- If the kids will eat beans and chips then dads will feed them it every day. And I mean every day . . .

Minor things in the grand scale. As one mother said to me: 'I'd love him to shape up, I'd hate him to ship out!'

When they do ship out . . .

It's a pretty dismal statistic that two out of three marriages collapse. This doesn't include unmarried parents where relationships come to an end. Often there's hurt, but contrary to popular legend there are a huge number of dads who are desperate to maintain contact with their children whatever the personal cost. One example is the ex of a friend of mine. Although an irritating husband, he's a dad devoted to his children. He lives for their weekends together and endures a life of loneliness and comparative poverty in this country. Were he to return to his well-to-do family in Pakistan he would have a wonderful life as opposed to the one he endures in England – bad weather and all excess income spent on child support.

There are of course many fathers who apparently have little qualms about cutting loose and abandoning their children but they are not as great in number as those who soldier on desperately trying to stay involved in their children's lives. The law is generally on the side of the mothers, particularly in cases where the parents are not married. Children

are often an easy pawn in relationships and it is understandable where a woman has been hurt that she will use whatever tools are available to hurt back. Bad-mouthing dad to the kids is often considered a fair weapon in a bitter war. This can eventually lead to the disintegration of the father-child relationship.

Statistically, a very high proportion of marriages break up where there is a disabled child involved. Once again the simple face-value explanation is that dads are wimps and abandon the sinking ship without a thought. But often families are placed under such stress by the failure of Local Education Authorities, Social Services and other so-called support agencies that the pressures become too great for the family to survive. The desperate dad of an autistic child told me that the Local Education Authority refused to fund a home educational programme, proffering instead a highly unsuitable school. He left the family home so that the child's mother could get benefits to pay for rent and living expenses. Meantime he moved in with his brother and ploughed all his earnings into paying for the child's programme.

The simple fact is that most fathers love their children to distraction and there is a dawning of a new age where men are unashamedly frank about these feelings. This is illustrated by a 2000 Harris Poll which found that 'young men in their twenties are seven times more likely than young women to give up pay for more time with their families'. Kudos to the modern dad!

- The above information is from *Families* magazine's web site: www.familiesmagazine.co.uk

© Families

Dads, stepdads and new partners

Information from Parentline Plus

Dads really do matter. Children need fathers as well as mothers and they need both men and women around them. Men are role models for what it means to be male, and can provide children with support, encouragement, and enjoyment.

Stepfathers or new partners are not substitute dads – there is no substitute. But they are additional adult men for children to relate to, which can be a real advantage for the children.

Thoughts

- Spend time alone with the children.
- Do things together that you both enjoy. These can be routine things like cooking together, watching and playing sports together or going out together. They can also be some more special times.
- Be available to the children during quiet times. This gives them a chance to talk to you.
- Keep your promises. Don't make promises you can't keep.
- Enjoy your children for who they are. Praise them for just being them.
- Enjoy your children for what they can do and praise them for what they do.
- Never wish that they were different or could do more.
- Let your children get to know you, too. Let them see who you are and what you can do, so that they can appreciate you.

Do you feel unsure of how you are doing? Or do you simply want more information on how to support your children in their daily lives? Why not look at some of our publications? Alternatively you can ring the Parentline Plus helpline free on 0808 800 2222 to talk about it.

Parentline plus

New dad

'I didn't really know my Dad when I was a kid. He wasn't around much, and when he was there we never really talked or did things together. Now I'm a Dad I want my children to know me – but I'm not sure how to do that.'

Becoming a dad may mean you reflect on your own relationship with your father and think about how you would like your relationship to be with your own child. If you haven't done already it may be worth sharing some of this with your partner so you can both check out your attitudes to bringing up children. If you are no longer with the mother of your child this may not be so easy but you can let her know your commitment to the child and that you want to be involved.

Being a parent

'I sometimes feel I'm living with creatures from another planet. I don't understand how they think. The things they say and do amaze me. It's fun, but it's really confusing.'

Babies don't come with instructions, there is no right way of doing things – you and your baby's mother will need to find what is best for you.

If it is the first child for your partner too, it does not mean that she has any more advantage or knowledge than you on how to parent. Whether you are together or not, talk about how you can share the care of your child, and talk about this again sometime after the birth. The reality may be different from what you expected and plans may need to be adjusted.

Money

It will come as no surprise that babies mean spending more money. Try to prepare as much as you can – build up a bit of cash if you can, find out from friends and relatives if they have prams or cots no longer in use, as well as clothes. It may also be worth trying to find out about any welfare benefits you may be entitled to. You could try www.dss.gov.uk or www.inlandrevenue.gov.uk

> *You should realise
> that your appearance
> on the scene may be hard
> for the children to come
> to terms with*

Sleep

You're probably well aware of the effect that less sleep will have on you. Try to work out with your partner opportunities for breaks – either time to sleep or time to get out of the house.

Time together

If you and your partner are living together, try to spend time together on your own now and again. This time will be a chance to catch up as well as being a break.

But spending time together as a family with your new child or children is also important.

Lifestyle changes

A new baby will change the way you do things. The more you and the baby's mum can share care, the more likely you will both adjust to being parents at the same pace. It will be important to let each other know how you feel, especially when things seem overwhelming. Parenting isn't easy.

Being able to tell each other about anger, resentment and the less pleasant feelings of being a parent is as important as telling each other about the rewards. For example, you may feel your partner is not letting you get involved as much as you would like, and this may make you feel resentful . Let her know by saying 'I feel . . . ' rather than sounding like you're blaming her . . . 'you should…'.

Attitudes

You may find that you and your partner have different values about bringing up children. Try to talk about these and find compromises. If conflict persists you could try some sessions with Relate: www.relate.org.uk

Living apart from your children

- Even if you don't live with your children, you still matter to them.
- Keep in touch. Use postcards, e-mails, telephone calls and if possible, make regular visits.
- Let them know that they matter to you.
- When your children come to visit you don't just try to do special things. They will appreciate doing ordinary, routine things too.
- Bear in mind that your children will have their own lives in their home – including friends, school, hobbies and so on. Don't be too rigid about visits, and let them have their say – especially as they get older.

Stepfathers and new partners

Being a stepfather is not the same as being a father, and being in a new family means that you will need to find a new role.

- You may want to reassure the children. For instance, let them know that you are not trying to replace their father. Instead, you are an additional adult in their lives they can turn to if they want to.
- Don't attempt discipline too soon. Build relationships with the children first.
- Treat all children fairly – your own and your stepchildren.
- You should realise that your appearance on the scene may be hard for the children to come to terms with. For example, they may believe that their parents will get back together – and they see you as the obstacle to this. Or they may be jealous that you are taking their mother's time and attention away from them.
- Give it time. It can take from 2 to 10 years for stepfamily relationships to settle.
- Talk to other men who are going through similar things. You will discover that you are not alone – and you may get some useful ideas of how other people have managed.

■ The above information is from the Parentline Plus web site: www.parentlineplus.org.uk

© Parentline Plus

How fathers fit into the family

The family system

Social scientists often emphasise the role of fathers in the family system, and how their actions affect the entire environment and context in which a child grows. One of the most important ways a father influences that environment is in his interaction with his children's mother. This is because the relationships which children observe and experience at an early age influence their own relationships later in life. It is also because family relationships are interrelated – the way that mothers and fathers interact affects the mother-child relationship as well as the father-child relationship. Because of this interrelatedness, parents who have a strong and happy relationship have a head start to being good parents.

Non-resident fathers

Statistics about children who do not live with their fathers can be grim. On almost every outcome that has been tested, including educational achievement, self-esteem, responsible social behaviour, and adjustment as adults, children do better when they live with both of their parents. Family instability and financial problems do contribute to the poor outcomes for children from broken homes. However, as one scholar who reviewed 28 studies of father absence states: 'the major disadvantage related to father absence for children is lessened parental attention'.

Non-resident fathers can face special challenges in contributing positively to their children's development. Fathers who do not live with their children simply are less available to nurture, guide, and provide for their children. In cases of divorce, some mothers limit the time children have with their fathers. Fathers who were never married are even less likely than divorced fathers to keep in contact with their children. Moreover, the large geographic distances that exist between some children and their fathers make close relationships difficult to maintain. Either parent or both may form new relationships and have children with other people. In many cases, the entire family enjoys a lower standard of living when they live apart.

Despite these disadvantages, non-resident fathers can still make a difference for their children. The most obvious route of influence is by providing adequate financial support. Studies show children whose fathers pay child support do better in school and have fewer behaviour problems. Children who feel close to their non-resident fathers also tend to do better. And, when non-resident fathers are able to use their time with their children wisely by helping with homework, setting and enforcing rules, and supervising their children, children can benefit a great deal.

Married or cohabiting fathers

The role of marriage as a foundation for family life has become controversial. More and more people are cohabiting or living together before marriage or as an alternative to marriage. More couples also are having children without marrying. Some people say that marriage is 'just a piece of paper' and does not make any difference to the couple or their children. For some couples, this might be the case. However, studies have shown that the majority of cohabiting couples are less committed than married couples, even if they have children. In fact, only 36% of children born to cohabiting couples are likely to live with both their mother and their father for their entire childhood, compared to 70% of children born within marriage. It is for this reason that many supporters of the father's role in raising children also support marriage for fathers.

Good fathering is good parenting

Most children do best when their mothers and fathers engage in what developmental psychologists call authoritative parenting. This style of parenting involves spending time with children, providing emotional support, giving everyday assistance, monitoring children's behaviour, and providing consistent, fair and proportionate discipline. This can be contrasted with permissive parenting, in which parents avoid setting standards and limits, and authoritarian parenting, in which parents are harsh and rigid in their discipline and fail to respect their child's point of view. Neither of these parenting styles have as positive an influence on children's development as authoritative parenting. Authoritative, or 'good parenting', may be expressed in different styles. While mothers tend to provide more emotional warmth for their children, fathers provide a strong sense of security. While children usually can depend on their mothers for unconditional love, they often must earn their father's approval. While mothers soothe their children more often, fathers often provide more stimulation. All parents – both mothers and fathers – have important roles in rearing their children. Better appreciation of where fathers fit in will lead to happier and more productive children.

■ The above information is from Civitas: the Institute for the Study of Civil Society's web site which can be found at www.civitas.org.uk

> *Fathers who do not live with their children simply are less available to nurture, guide, and provide for their children*

Being a home-dad

More and more of us are taking up the option of staying at home full time to look after the children. Whether it's because mum earns more, or because looking after children just seems like a better option than working, it's a big job with little respect and no pay. Debbie Giggle looks at the issues facing dads who care for their kids full time

Approximately 17 fathers in every 1,000 in the UK stay at home while their partners work – so that means there are around 110,000 full-time dads in Britain. The figures have increased dramatically in a time of economic growth. For whatever reason they come to it, lots of dads are choosing to stay at home to look after their children. In the US, the figure is something like two million.

But if you spent a few days pushing a buggy round the shopping centre and down to the park it would be easy to think that you were the only man on earth doing this job! And that's where this article fits in. We hope that you will contact us with your views and advice for new recruits who are navigating their way through the first few months in the Great Indoors.

In this section, we tackle one of the drawbacks of full-time fatherhood – isolation. Parenting can be isolating for mums, too, but for dads support can often be thin on the ground.

We British pride ourselves on flying solo. If you circumnavigate the globe single-handedly, or scale Everest without a sherpa, then the world and his brother will turn out to welcome you home. But when you work at home – and childcare is certainly a job to take pride in – no one sees you out there.

As well as the lack of recognition, part of the reality of bringing up a small child is that without the odd bit of adult conversation you can find yourself climbing the walls! Some feel comfortable with the situation, but others find that the absence of contact with the outside world can make the otherwise enjoyable experience of being at home with the children a rather lonely time. You might also reckon that your child could do with mucking in with other kids from time to time.

So how do you get round feeling as if both you and your kids (or just you) have stepped off the world? Here are a few suggestions, but we hope you'll also start off some discussions with your views and ideas.

Make sure you know whether there's anything going on for parents and dads in your area. Sometimes you have to do a bit of research before you turn up anything interesting. Ask around. If no one else knows, the baby clinic staff at the local surgery always have their ears to the ground. Ask the health visitor, or midwife if she visits. Don't let them ignore you. Let them understand you are involved. Leisure centres have play zones for kids and young toddlers. Try the Internet.

If you draw a blank – then you may have to make it happen! If you are too embarrassed to ask a mum home for tea for your children to play together, then try asking two! This takes guts – but at least this way everybody can see there is nothing funny going on.

Take a deep breath and try out the local playgroup or parent and toddler group – even if it is still called 'mums-and-tots'. If you have a toddler they will appreciate the new stimulus, and you might even enjoy it yourself. The National Childbirth Trust may be able to suggest a group.

Remember that it takes time to be accepted by any group of people, so don't put down feeling isolated at first just to being a man. Remember the mums come to the group because they feel isolated at home, too: it's a group, not a gang. If they see you are there to give your child some social interaction, they will know what you are about, because that's why they are there too. You have being a parent in common and that is something you can share.

Consider all your babysitting options. As much as we love our kids, they benefit most if we have a life outside them. The temptation is to transfer the same single-minded focus you had for your job onto your family – and that's not good!! Find some space. Work off the frustrations at the gym.

Keep the channels of communication open. Don't sever links with friends and old colleagues. They'll take their lead from you. If

you never phone they will just assume you're too busy to meet up. Don't feel your worlds are too different, either. If they are in full-time jobs, the truth is they will probably envy your chance to be with your kids and really know them. At least privately they will respect your commitment to bringing up your kids well. But men are often reluctant to say these things. Here's what some dads say about it.

'Because people see me around the house and in the village during the day they assume I have nothing to do. In fact, I'm rushed off my feet working from home.'
Graham, primary carer for Samantha (12).

'My local Mums & Tots was like the Japanese gameshow Endurance. Some men feel really comfortable around women but it didn't suit me at all.'
Mark, full-time dad of Karen, aged 6.

'I used to spend a lot of time with my next-door neighbour, but her husband thought I was up to something so I decided to give that a wide swerve! I kept my sanity by keeping up my rugby and going to the local pub for the odd game of pool.'
Sam, full-time dad of three.

'Playgroups are no problem. One woman started haranguing me once about how much she hated men, but apart from that I loved being surrounded by friendly young women!'
Paul, full-time dad for 7 years.

'I never used to worry about money before I started looking after Jack. I felt I didn't have as much control over our finances because there were limitations on my earnings. Feeling that you are not master of your own destiny is a bit alien.'
Simon, an antiques dealer who combines care of Jack (now aged 8) with self-employment.

■ The above information is from the Fathers Directs' web site which can be found at www.fathersdirect.com

Confident parenting

Information from Save the Children

Introduction
We all want to be good parents. But while it's usual to have lessons to learn to drive a car, somehow we're just expected to know how to bring up children.

Being a parent is one of the most demanding jobs we'll ever do. We've probably all had days when we're pushed to breaking point and we do or say things we regret. Or days when we're riddled with doubts about whether or not we're doing the right thing.

Rest assured, there's no such thing as a perfect parent. Nor is there one 'right' way to bring up your children. But there are ways that parenting can be easier and less fraught.

This article provides practical tips on how to take the stress out of parenting. It suggests ways to develop children's co-operation and self-discipline without resorting to smacking.

Confident parenting
Nobody wins if parenting is a continual battle, where parents force children to do as they are told. Children grow up feeling resentful or angry and parents are too stressed to enjoy their children.

Parenting is easiest when it's based on good communication. This works both ways. Children have the right to express themselves, learn and develop. But parents also have the right to set limits about what behaviour is OK and what isn't. This approach is called 'positive discipline'.

Positive discipline involves:
■ believing children want to communicate and co-operate
■ listening to them
■ discussing what you want them to do
■ setting clear limits for behaviour
■ being firm and consistent
■ looking at disagreements as an opportunity to develop problem-solving skills.

If children are listened to, their communication and negotiation skills will develop. They will learn to sort out arguments without threats or violence, because they learn from us how to negotiate.

It doesn't mean, however, that children should get everything they want. Sometimes they need to know that when you ask them to do something it's not up for debate. If children generally feel that they are listened to and their viewpoints respected, then when you are firm about something, they will respond well.

Through children's eyes
Save the Children asked 76 children aged between five and eight what they thought about smacking. Here's what they told us:
■ Smacking is really hitting. One girl said: 'Smacking is what parents do when they hit you, only they call it a smack.'
■ Smacking doesn't work. Children sometimes don't understand what they've done wrong or feel so overwhelmed by the hurt that they forget what they've done.
■ Smacking teaches children that hitting someone smaller and less powerful is OK. This is confusing if children are being smacked for hurting or hitting others.
■ Smacking is wrong.

■ The above information is from Save the Children's web site: www.savechildren.org.uk

Full-time mothers

A child's need – a mother's right

What the papers say

Among all the many items suitable for inclusion in this section a recurring theme recently has been on the lines of 'The death of Superwoman.' Several surveys have exposed the stress and exhaustion experienced in trying to live up to this image.

The *Daily Mail* ran a piece with just this title, stating 'For 30 years feminists have preached that women can have a family and a career. Now a survey reveals a huge majority would rather stay at home.' A reader wrote in to say she had found the article empowering, and it had helped her to reach her decision to leave her job of 14 years and be a stay-at-home mum.

'Working a lot of hours in the first year of a child's life is associated with poorer cognitive and verbal development'

The superwoman myth was further dented by a report in the *Sunday Times* entitled 'Working mothers' children do worse'. Detailed studies by American scientists showed that children whose mothers

returned to work within 9 months of giving birth did 10% less well in tests at the age of three. 'Working a lot of hours in the first year of a child's life is associated with poorer cognitive and verbal development,' said researcher Dr Jeanne Brooks-Gunn.

It was acknowledged that if parents feel they have no choice about working, babies do better with one-to-one care from grandparents, nannies or childminders rather than nurseries. The article goes on, 'nothing however fully compensates for a mother's absence' before quoting our own Alex Nightingale who, as a secondary school teacher, has not returned to the classroom since the first of her three children was born. 'I am lucky. My children are very observant. It is good for them that they can chat to you about things they have noticed when it occurs to them, rather than just in a crammed half-hour of forced contact at the end of the day when you are both tired.'

Long-hours cultures

All this notwithstanding, the *Daily Mail* recently reported an alarming increase in the long-hours culture; research has shown that one in eight women now works more than 60 hours a week – over double the number two years ago. Among men it is one in six.

Excessive hours are causing stress and ill-health, putting a strain on family life and cutting the time available for mothers to spend with their children. Even the Government is uneasy. A DTI spokesman said: 'We do have concerns about the steep rise in the number of women working these hours. Many will be working mothers and this will place stress on the family.'

Women under stress

Good Housekeeping magazine interviewed 1000 women between 30 and 55 for their June edition and discovered an alarmingly high level of stress; we all do too much, they found. In a piece entitled 'The stress epidemic: how it's destroying women's health, happiness and tearing at the very fabric of society' GH's editor-in-chief Lindsay Nicholson wrote: 'Many, perhaps the majority of women in Britain today, live in a permanent state of shattered

nerves and chronic fatigue. The effect of their health, their marriages, and on how they raise their children makes uncomfortable reading. It cannot be either wise or morally right for a civilised, rich western country to turn a blind eye to these appalling levels of stress and to allow so many of its citizens to feel like drudges.'

Many of the respondents said they were too stressed to make love, 40% had sleeping problems and 90% believed the increased opportunities available to women had put them under extra pressure.

Low birth rate

In May it was announced that the birth rate was at a record low, and at an average of 1.64 per woman, has dropped below the level considered as crucial in maintaining a balance between young and old. The long-term consequences could be grave, with growing strains on the economy as the tax burden rises.

Blame for this situation was placed by commentators on various things, from greater choice in contraception, and an increase in women having children late or choosing not to have them at all, to long working hours, few public holidays (the UK is 13 days behind the EU average), women's changed career aspirations, stress, and rising house prices. Allison Pearson, bemoaning in the *Evening Standard* the frantic pressure so many women live under, quoted a wise man she had met who had told her, 'Now children, Allison, children are the reward for living.'

Childcare options

In a report in the *Guardian* about preferred choice of childcare (mis-

---

The situation in the UK is hardly better; a slow realisation is dawning on the world, and that is that there is a huge price to pay for women who devoted themselves to the workplace

---

leadingly entitled 'Report says childminders more trusted than relatives'), a survey of 1200 families revealed that families chose child-minders before nurseries, finding them to be more welcoming, close and loving than the former. Of all outside carers, grand-parents were the most likely to be 'close and loving'. The reason for the headline was apparently that they were also more inclined to tell the mother when the child had been unhappy in a way that made her feel guilty. (!)

Children as home wreckers?

When an article from the *Sunday Times* was reported on in *The Week* under the heading 'Why children are home-wreckers' one angry ten-year-old wrote to *The Week* indignantly rebutting this assertion. The headline derived from a study of 25,000 British households which has found that parenthood has become a significant 'risk factor' for divorce.

In the Fifties, having a child reduced the chance of divorce by 16%; by the Nineties, however, it raised the risk by 37%. The older the child is, the greater the destabilising effect, lending some credence, said *The Week*, to those who argue that the cost of raising a child in today's consumer culture is putting an unbearable strain on marriages. Male earning power is apparently also a key influence on the success of a marriage. The higher a man's wages, the more likely the marriage will last, but if the wife earns significantly more than the husband, the re-searchers claimed that the probability of a divorce increases.

Last but not least in the under-mining of the superwoman concept came the publication of Sylvia Ann Hewlett's new book *Baby Hunger*. This book has terrified much of female America said *The Times*, by revealing to them that 49% of middle-aged high-achieving women are childless, and most not by choice. It shows how a generation of high-flying women have put careers before babies, and many of them have great regrets.

But the situation in the UK is hardly better; a slow realisation is dawning on the world, and that is that there is a huge price to pay for women who devoted themselves to the workplace. The statistics are frightening: only 3% of high-flying women marry for the first time after 35. Fertility drops by 50% from its peak level after the age of 35; after 40 it crashes by 95%.

The Times' coverage, run over several days, provoked some heart-rending letters from women who had left conception too late, and then found great difficulty in conceiving. One, who had finally after four years of harrowing treatment given birth to a son, wrote, 'I would not wish my worse enemy to experience the utter despair, longing, frustration and pain inherent in the ART process.' Someone else wrote, 'I've had so many fertility procedures I can't keep track of them. We've had to take out a second mortgage.' Another whose treatment had failed wrote of the relief of giving up a process so filled with anguish and yearning. Another wrote of how monumentally depressing she found the whole thing when she had done everything her generation were supposed to do – education, career, flat, relationships (which like jobs she felt she had no right to expect to last more than two years) – but still found that family and children had somehow been omitted.

■ The above information is from the Full Time Mothers web site: www.fulltimemothers.org

© *Full Time Mothers*

Does work pay?

A long-term study warns that working mums are bad for children. Jane Cunningham looks at the implications

As a mother, almost everything you do for yourself has a pay-back. You know, the girls' weekend away where you come back to more washing-up than you thought possible, hyper kids because Daddy/ Granny/Auntie didn't know that blue sweets set them off and a cross-legged dog desperate to be let out? Even half a day's shopping seems to have repercussions to the general well-being of the household. And it seems that working for a living is the ultimate way to wreck your child's chances of becoming chairman of the board and leave him emotionally poor and intellectually weak.

These gems come straight from a report by the Joseph Rowntree Foundation Family Policy Studies Centre, whose conclusions from a long-term study beginning in the seventies into the effects of parents' employment on children's lives should have us all running to the kitchen to make muffins and help with homework. Needless to say, the report finds that dads can broadly do as they please, workwise, without casting any shadows upon their children's development. (But see 'Dad about the house' box.)

> *'Long-term research is not necessarily relevant to children of today. In the fifties and sixties, when most women didn't work, children did not necessarily grow up to be high achievers'*

Many women have to work, for economic or sanity reasons, so reports like this are yet another way of damning mothers just for living in the modern world. We can't all be Nicola Horlicks, we don't all have choices about whether to work or not, and wanting to work, through choice or necessity, just shouldn't be so damn hard. The report helpfully states that part-time employment can lessen the impact on children, but try telling that to a single mum supporting three kids and a mortgage. Just so we all know exactly what is being levelled at us, the (selected) conclusions of the report are as follows:

Long periods of full-time employment by mothers with children aged one to five:
- reduce the child's educational attainment
- increase the risk of unemployment and economic inactivity in early adulthood
- increase the risk of experiencing psychological distress as a young adult

Mothers who work part-time, with children aged one to five:
- reduce the child's educational attainment (but the effect is less marked than in those with mothers in full-time employment)
- reduce the risk of later psychological distress.

Child psychologist Jennie Lindon puts things in perspective: 'Long-term research is not necessarily relevant to children of today. In the fifties and sixties, when most women didn't work, children did not necessarily grow up to be high achievers.' She stresses, however, 'If parents are completely absorbed in their careers, it can mess their kids up. Children can't be slotted in like meetings, and relationships will crack around the edges if too little time is spent as a family.'

Educationally, do teachers see a difference in the classroom between children with both parents working and those with mothers at home? Educational psychologist Hilary Scott, whose work brings her into contact with children from a wide variety of home circumstances, says:

'My gut feeling is that there is no discernable difference, and certainly not a marked one. It's not as if I have swaths of children with working mothers referred to me.' Hilary's mother worked when she was a child. 'I was really proud of my mum,' she says. 'We were typical latch-key kids, but it never occurred to me as an adult not to work.'

Naturally, there are counter reports that suggest kids are better off for having working mothers as strong role models, particularly when those women work part-time. And children don't necessarily suffer a negative impact from the socialisation, independence and confidence they may gain from their childcare experiences. What the report doesn't take fully into account is the personalities of individual children, the quality of parenting they receive when their parents are at home and the many recent permutations of childcare from all-day nursery care to being looked after for a couple of hours by their granny. Nor does the report take into account differing qualities of childcare.

Of course women with children have the right to work – it's downright unfair that talented, hard-working, ambitious mothers have searing guilt trips laid upon them by academics and statisticians. But the hard truth of the matter is that if the seemingly endless series of reports are right, the impact on our children when we work does have some negative aspects. Part of being a parent is making difficult choices and living with the consequences. It's not great, it's not fair and it's hard to swallow, but then, 21st-century living was never going to be a cakewalk. Jennie Lindon sums it up: 'The bottom line is, do your best, give your kids as much time and attention as you can spare and love them. Supermum is a myth; you can't have it all.'

So, if we work, is there a way to ensure our kids don't fall into the categories of the study's findings?

- Give your kids time, time and more time – as much as you can spare

---

Of course women with children have the right to work – it's downright unfair that talented, hard-working, ambitious mothers have searing guilt trips laid upon them by academics and statisticians

---

- Consistency is important to children – if carers come and go, your children will feel unsettled
- Your children will accept expensive presents, but they'd much rather have you
- In two-parent families, try to divide the domestic chores equally
- Do listen and take seriously any worries your children have regarding their childcare
- Early years are important; you can't put your kids on hold, but you may be able to downshift your career for a while
- If there is spare cash, spend it on a cleaner, gardener or ironer –

Dad about the house

At the latest count, there are now more stay-at-home dads than ever, with one in roughly every 20 households. And, given the statistic that, by the year 2020, women will account for half of the main breadwinners in two-adult households, this figure is bound to rise. So can we mums feel okay about working if we know dad is at home? According to an eight-year study by psychologists Kyle Puett and Brian Litzenberger of Yale University in the US, the answer is yes. However, we're not completely off the hook: they emphasise that children benefit most from a 'parenting partnership', with input from mum and dad.

anyone who can lift the domestic chores off your shoulders, leaving more family time

- Find the right childcare; if you have any niggles or doubts, have a rethink

The Effects of Parents' Employment on Children's Lives by John Ermisch and Marco Francesconi, £10.95, tel. 020 7388 5900.

How was it for you?

Emma Jackson, 35, from York, works as a nursery nurse and has two children, Hannah, 11, and Edward, eight. 'The children say they don't mind me working, but I do feel that Hannah begrudes it – or maybe I feel guilty. She minds me missing speech day and sports day – but I mind that too. I don't work during the school holidays so I don't have any worries about childcare during that time, but I couldn't work without the support of my husband, John, who is a farmer and can pick up the children occasionally. If I didn't have the holidays off, life would be a nightmare. I know I can spend that time with the children and enjoy it. Since I started working, I've instigated a "family tea" so that every day we have a time to be together.'

Diane Staplehurst, from Liverpool, aged 36, has two children, Ruby, nine, and Teddy, five. She works part-time in PR for a large retail company. 'I really resented my mum working because I wanted her to be home when I got in from school, baking cakes and looking after me. I wanted a roly-poly mum who was always there and she wasn't. I work part-time and pick up my children from school. I take my work holiday during the school holidays and, because my husband does shift work, we juggle things around so one of us is always available – even if the kids do just ignore us! Me working has virtually no impact on my children's lives.'

- The above information is from *Right Start* magazine's web site which can be found at www.rightstartmagazine.co.uk

The advantages of being an older parent

By Jan Anderson

When I first published my light-hearted and inspirational account of pregnancy and birth at the age of 40, I received tremendous feedback from older women (and men) from all over the world. Indeed, even now, I receive many wonderful e-mails every week from women over the age of 35 who are either planning a family, are already pregnant, or who themselves have had a baby over the age of 40. The article had offered hope, encouragement and reassurance in a world that seems otherwise to be filled with negative statistics and horror stories about being an older mother. It also highlighted the fact that far from being unusual, tens of thousands of women across the globe are becoming, what is affectionately known as, 'older parents'.

> *Tens of thousands of women across the globe are becoming, what is affectionately known as, 'older parents'*

Currently, one out of every five women worldwide is delaying having her first baby until the age of 35, a number that is rising steadily, together with the growing trend for middle-aged women to add to their existing family. There are many reasons why a woman chooses to have a baby in her forties; the establishment of a career before embarking on parenthood, for example, or a woman who has re-married and wishes to have a child with her new partner. Despite this, there still seems to be very little optimistic information available that is specific to midlife mothers. The focus definitely needs to shift towards the positive aspects of midlife parenting, particularly since medical studies have established that there is little added risk for a healthy woman in her forties embarking on motherhood.

In my communications with other older mothers, several questions were raised, one of the most common being, 'Will my child object to having older parents?' I think that this question highlighted the assumption of many that old age goes hand-in-hand with ill health and incapacity and yet this is not necessarily so. You can be an unhealthy 25-year-old parent and a vital, energetic 75-year-old grandparent. You can also become sick at any age, so don't assume that just because you don't have a child until you are in your forties, you won't be around to see your son or daughter when he or she grows up. Besides, it is quality of time and not quantity that is the most important and a child who is brought into a secure and loving environment by a middle-aged couple, is more likely to thrive than a child brought into an unstable home by young parents.

I interviewed several people who were raised by older parents, one of whom is an older parent herself and all of whom kindly allowed me to share their stories with you.

Jacqueline's mother was 43 and her father was 48 when Jacqueline was born. Jacqueline, now 42, says, 'I never once regretted having older parents. Whilst they were really strict, they were also very fair and because they were older and wiser they had a greater sense of the important values in life. Younger people are often still too self-obsessed and unsure of their path in life, so it can be difficult for them to offer a true sense of security or to give their all to a child because they are still like so vulnerable themselves.

'I didn't follow in my mother's footsteps because I was only 26 when I had my son, and yet in retrospect I don't really think that I was prepared for motherhood. Don't misunderstand me, I love my son to bits and don't ever regret having him, but if I could turn back time and have the opportunity to make different choices, I think that I would have waited until at least my mid thirties before starting a family. Oddly enough, my husband and I have recently been discussing the possibility of having another child and having had an older mother myself makes me feel so much more comfortable about midlife parenting.

'I respected my parents enormously and they respected me, something that I noticed was lacking in some of my friends' homes. If I was not permitted to do something, my parents would clearly explain why not, whereas many of my friends with younger parents would simply be told, "Because I said so, that's why".

'With a twenty-year marriage behind them, my parents had managed to resolve any of their differences early on. Many of my school friends lived in homes where it was commonplace for the parents to be at each other's throats constantly and to think nothing of openly belittling each other in front of the children. What sort of message does that pass on to children about love and marriage?

ADDITIONAL RESOURCES

You might like to contact the following organisations for further information. Due to the increasing cost of postage, many organisations cannot respond to enquiries unless they receive a stamped, addressed envelope.

Economic and Social Research Council (ESRC)
Polaris House
North Star Avenue
Swindon
Wiltshire, SN2 1UJ
Tel: 01793 413000
Fax: 01793 413130
E-mail: exrel@esrc.ac.uk
Web site: www.esrc.ac.uk or www.regard.ac.uk
The ESRC is the UK's largest independent funding agency for research and postgraduate training in social and economic issues.

Families
PO Box 4302
London, SW16 1ZS
Tel: 020 8696 9680
Fax: 020 8696 9679
E-mail: info@familiesmagazine.co.uk
Web site: www.familiesmagazine.co.uk
Families® is a free magazine available in printed form throughout the areas we cover, as well as online on this website, or by post on subscription. Packed full of everything of interest to parents with young children, the printed editions include advertisements for local suppliers in each area.

Fathers Direct
Herald House
15 Lamb's Passage
Bunhill Row
London, EC1Y 8TQ
Tel: 020 7920 9491
Fax: 020 7374 2966
Web site: www.fathersdirect.com
Fathers Direct is the national information centre for fatherhood. They work to ensure that children, particularly socially deprived children, get the best possible love and care from their fathers.

Full Time Mothers
PO Box 186
London, SW3 5RF
Tel: 020 8670 2525
E-mail: fulltimemothers@hotmail.com
Web site: www.fulltimemothers.org
Full Time Mothers aims to promote understanding of the child's need for a full-time mother, enhance the status and self-esteem of mothers at home, campaign for changes in the tax and benefits system and to employment policy, in order to give more women the choice to be full-time mothers.

The Future Foundation
First Floor
70 Cowcross Street
London, EC1M 6DG
Tel: 020 7250 3343
Fax: 020 7251 8138
E-mail: info@futurefoundation.net
Web site: www.futurefoundation.net
The Future Foundation is a business-focused think-tank set up in July 1996 which aims to help organisations improve their performance through understanding, anticipating and responding to their customers.

National Family and Parenting Institute (NFPI)
430 Highgate Studios
58-79 Highgate Road
London, NW5 1TL
Tel: 020 7424 3460
Fax: 020 7424 3590
E-mail: info@nfpi.org
Web site: www.nfpi.org and www.e-parents.org
An independent charity working to improve the lives of parents and families by campaigning for a more family-friendly society.

Parentline Plus
Unit 520 Highgate Studios
53-57 Highgate Road
London, NW5 1TL
Tel: 020 7284 5500
Fax: 020 7284 5501
E-mail: centraloffice@parentlineplus.org.uk
Web site: www.parentlineplus.org.uk
A national helpline for parents under stress. They run a series of telephone helplines. Parentline is the national freephone helpline run by Parentline Plus. Contact Parentline on 0808 800 2222 Monday - Friday 9am-9pm, Saturdays 9.30am-5pm and Sundays 10am-3pm. Text phone: 0800 783 6783.

Save the Children
17 Grove Lane
Camberwell
London, SE5 8RD
Tel: 020 7703 5400
Fax: 020 7703 2278
E-mail: enquiries@scfuk.org.uk
Web site: www.savethechildren.org.uk
www.savethechildren.org.uk/rightonline
www.savethechildren.org.uk/education and www.beatpoverty.org
Save the Children is the leading UK charity working to create a better world for children. We work in 70 countries helping children in the world's most impoverished communities. We are part of the International Save the Children Alliance, which aims to be a truly international movement for children. Produce a wide range of materials. Ask for the catalogue.

INDEX

ACKNOWLEDGEMENTS

The publisher is grateful for permission to reproduce the following material.

While every care has been taken to trace and acknowledge copyright, the publisher tenders its apology for any accidental infringement or where copyright has proved untraceable. The publisher would be pleased to come to a suitable arrangement in any such case with the rightful owner.

Chapter One: Families in the UK Today

What makes a family today?, © Jill Curtis, *The changing face of UK families*, © Rachael Crofts, Press Association Features, *Households by size*, © Crown copyright is reproduced with the permission of Her Majesty's Stationery Office, *Birth rate drops to the lowest on record*, © The Daily Mail, December 2002, *Diverse family forms across Europe*, © Economic and Social Research Council (ESRC), *Households by type*, © Crown copyright is reproduced with the permission of Her Majesty's Stationery Office, *Nuclear family goes into meltdown*, © Guardian Newspapers Limited 2002, *Births outside marriage rise to 40%*, © Guardian Newspapers Limited 2002, *Does Britain really like its children?*, © McMillan Scott plc, *Families and work*, © National Family & Parenting Institute, *Experiments in living*, © Civitas: the Institute for the Study of Civil Society, *How do fathers fit in?*, © Civitas: the Institute for the Study of Civil Society, *Average age at first marriage*, ©

Crown copyright is reproduced with the permission of Her Majesty's Stationery Office, *Stepfamilies*, © Parentline Plus, *Grannies and Gramps*, © Families, *Double act*, © Children's Express.

Chapter Two: Parenting Issues

Being a parent today, © Jill Curtis, *Listening to parents*, © National Family & Parenting Institute, *Stressed parents*, © Guardian Newspapers Limited 2002, *Nine steps to more effective parenting*, © KidsHealth, *Get with the programme*, © Guardian Newspapers Limited 2002, *A father writes: parenting*, © Telegraph Group Limited, London 2003, *Dads rule OK*, © Families, *Dads, stepdads and new partners*, © Parentline Plus, *How fathers fit into the family*, © Civitas: the Institute for the Study of Civil Society, *Being a home-dad*, © Fathers Direct, *Confident parenting*, © Save the Children, *Full-time mothers*, © Full Time Mothers, *Does work pay?*, © McMillan Scott plc, *The advantages of being an older parent*, © UK Families Ltd, *All work and no playtime*, © Guardian Newspapers Limited 2002, *Parenting alone*, © TheSite.org.

Photographs and illustrations:

Pages 1, 18, 22, 30, 35: Bev Aisbett; pages 3, 9, 16, 19, 23, 28, 32, 38: Simon Kneebone; pages 7, 17, 27: Pumpkin House.

Craig Donnellan
Cambridge
May, 2003